UNCOVERING BIBLE TIMES

A Study in Biblical Archeology

BY

MERRILL T. GILBERTSON

AUGSBURG PUBLISHING HOUSE
Minneapolis, Minnesota

UNCOVERING BIBLE TIMES

Scripture quotations are from the Revised Standard Version

This book is lovingly

dedicated

to my faithful Bible students

in

Grace Lutheran Church

Albert Lea, Minnesota

and

First Lutheran Church

Columbia Heights, Minnesota

CONTENTS

Illustrations: Insert section following page 74

CHAPTER ONE

Introduction to Archeology

To many people the word "archeology" suggests something tinder-dry, dusty, and uninteresting, but to others the term is full of excitement and romance, suggesting buried treasure, hidden cities, or great discoveries. In reality, though, neither of these stereotypes is true. Archeology, very simply, is a study of the old objects created by the human mind and hand which have been found in the earth's crust. It is a study of man's material possessions, such as letters, utensils, pottery, temples, homes, and cities; in a wider sense, it involves the investigation and comprehension of ancient civilizations in order to reconstruct their history, rise, growth, and fall.

Archeology has developed into an exact science requiring great skill, patience, and tedious toil. Startling discoveries are occasionally made, but more often spectacular results do not arise. The real search of the archeologist is not for the wealth or fame but simply for knowledge about a certain phase of history. He accomplishes this by carefully piecing together evidences which will deepen the understanding of an age, a race, or a culture.

The special task of biblical archeology is to discover the remains of the past in the Bible lands, to recognize their value, and to fit the data together in a coherent picture of the whole. The biblical archeologist is interested in probing the mystery of those great vanished civilizations through which promises of the Scriptures were fulfilled. In his search he studies such things as the writings on tombstones, the figures on a vase, the dates on a coin, or the paintings on the wall of a temple. Gradually, after painstaking care, he can recreate a picture of the way people lived in Bible times.

We should probably ask at the outset how the ruins archeologists investigate came to be. How did cities become buried, lost, or forgotten? Both men and nature have had curious ways of making this happen.

Man himself has been responsible for many of these catastrophes by destroying cities, obliterating entire civilizations, and building up new cultures. Assyria, Babylon, Persia, Greece, and Rome each fought in turn for the right to control the Holy Land, for it is at the crossroads of the three continents of Europe, Asia, and Africa. Every major war in history has left its mark on the Bible lands.

The ancient cycle of civilization in a city often took place in this way: When an enemy captured the city he would often tear it down or set the torch to it. The old residents of the city would be killed, carried away as slaves, or left to rebuild a new home. In the course of time a new city might be built. Some cities, however, were never rebuilt. Even if the site was desirable, it was usually easier to build the new city upon the foundations of the old.

The people of Palestine always chose to build their

cities upon hills, in order to gain some protection from their enemies. Since natural sites for cities are not plentiful in Palestine, the most desirable site which could be found was often the one on which a destroyed city once stood. The old ruins could be leveled off and the unbroken stones used over again. Sometimes the rubble of the old city was not even carried away or cleaned up; the old foundations were used in the construction of the new city.

This cycle of destruction was repeated so often that the site of most biblical cities, after many centuries, became a mound of sand, dirt, and rubble which archeologists called a "tell." ("Tell" is an Arabic word for hill, used to describe the mounds of a covered city.) The remains of the former city usually form a "stratum" or "layer of occupation" within a tell of five to seven or more feet in depth, with each successive city located higher than the former one.[1] These "layers" or levels must be handled and studied carefully, since each layer represents a different culture.

An interesting example of this ancient form of urban redevelopment is the city of Bethshan, which lies 14 miles south of the Sea of Galilee; it was the city to which Saul's body was taken after his suicide in the battle against the Philistines at Mount Gilboa (1 Sam. 31:8-10). Bethshan was excavated by an archeologist from the University of Pennsylvania in 1921-1933. The archeologist dug down over 70 feet, through 18 distinct "layers of occupation"; beneath these layers he found pits of unknown origin. The history of the city may have begun as early as 3500 B.C. and continued through Bible times.[2]

Not all cities, however, were destroyed by man; the forces of nature also took their toll of cities in Palestine. Earthquakes are common to this area; fires often destroyed a city; storms added their devastation; pestilence and disease depopulated cities and left the sites to natural decay and deterioration; fierce sirocco winds carried with them tons of sand and dust which, in time, buried abandoned cities. When other peoples came to construct a new city on an old site, their refuse and debris, which was usually in the streets, added to the materials that were stratified in the layers. As a result of all of these natural processes, many of the sites upon which the people of the Bible built their cities grew as much as five to seven feet every hundred years.

When cities of the past were buried by nature, destroyed by man, or obliterated by calamity, the memory of their location easily became lost. But man, like nature, also preserved, unknowingly, the culture of the past, and on these kinds of remains the archeologist bases much of his work. Inscriptions carved on tombs, monuments, and temples all tell stories of past glory, war, or achievement. Artists and craftsmen have vivid records of their cultures in their designs, paintings, pottery, and sculpture. Clay tablets have given many insights into the life of the Bible land people. Historians kept their records for the use of the archeologist. Old maps and geographies are valuable aids in opening the gaps and vistas of the past.

Another factor favoring the archeologist is that much of the Bible lands lies in regions which have been arid, sandy, and desolate. This has helped to preserve many ancient records. The dry sands of Palestine, Egypt, Babylon, Assyria, and Persia have covered and carefully preserved ancient cities, tombs, temples, palaces, libraries, schools, and market places. These sands have also proved to be a good means of protecting such remains as mummies, rolls of papyrus, furniture, pottery, and household furnishings.

Archeology through the years has had a rocky history.

Up until recent times the main motive of excavation was loot and not learning. Souvenir hunters scooped up their discoveries and carried away valuable antiquities to adorn their homes, courtyards, and libraries. Grave robbers were interested only in hidden treasure. The world lost much valuable information through such careless and willful destruction. After a site has once been sacked, it is almost impossible for the concerned archeologist to make a thorough study of its significance.

The age which had the first real historical interest in the past (and not merely a desire for plunder) was called the Renaissance. A cross-cultural movement which began in the 14th century, it was an age of great opportunity and rapid advancement in many fields. The printing press, world trade, increased scholarly activity, and newly acquired wealth in an economy based on money and not barter encouraged a growing interest in the past. Rich families of Europe ornamented their palaces with precious art, marble statues, pottery, gems, and coins from the ancient world. The villas of the wealthy became the first museums to house the treasures of the past.

Soon it became increasingly difficult to find such antiquities as men desired on the open ground. Men were forced to dig in the earth in order to find articles from the past to adorn the palaces of the rich. Men of means vied with one another to increase their collection of the world's art. Digging for the past became a popular and fashionable pastime.

Digging led to the writing of books, to discussions, and to debate. It was not long before the wealthy became amateur archeologists. Archeological societies were formed in all the capitals of the world. Organized expeditions were sent out on a large scale to dig in the ruins of cities, temples, tombs, public buildings, and private homes to fill the museums of Europe with artifacts from the Bible lands. Techniques of excavation and for the drawing and recording of the finds of archeologists were soon developed.

Napoleon the Great included in his army a group of 100 geographers, scientists, and skilled draftsmen, whose duty it was to collect and study antiquities systematically and to write careful accounts of them. It was an officer of Napoleon's French army of occupation who, in 1799, discovered a most unusual stone near Rosetta, Egypt.

The so-called "Rosetta Stone" was a slab of black basalt three and one-half feet long, two and one-half feet wide, and nearly a foot thick. The stone had been erected in 195 B.C. by priests in Egypt in honor of Ptolemy Epiphanes. On its surface was the same inscription in three different languages: Greek, hieroglyphics, and the common language of the untutored Egyptian people. Since the Greek of that time could still easily be read, three corresponding texts enabled scholars to decipher the other inscriptions on the stone. The Rosetta stone furnished the key for reading all the hieroglyphics of Egypt.

In the 19th century Britain, the Netherlands, Italy, and Germany became interested in archeology, and each nation made contributions to the growing science. Their archeologists developed new and scientific means of digging; they kept minute records of all their diggings, so that everything found could be reconstructed on paper. As Dr. Mortimer Wheeler, an eminent archeologist, once said, "Sweating with the pen is no less important than sweating with the spade." By painstaking and methodical work, centuries of ignorance about entire civilizations of the Bible lands began to crumble.

Today the study of the Scripture is much more meaningful because of the discoveries of biblical archeology. As a result of archeologists' painstaking work, much has been made more clear about the way the people of the Bible worshiped, the type of houses they lived in, the cities they built, the cultures they developed, and their trade and travels. The physical environments of these peoples have been established by discovering the kind of climate that was prevalent, what crops they raised, what wild or domestic animals they owned, and the foods they ate.

It is, however, a long step from the chaotic mound of a buried city to a clear picture of what life in that city was like. The archeologist must fit together many different kinds of pieces before the puzzle even begins to make sense. Let us look at the kinds of remains an archeologist works with; by doing so we may come to appreciate both the difficulties and the fascination of his job.

First of all, archeologists work with the remains of once-living things.

The identification of animals is not difficult, for the bones can be put together and the missing parts reconstructed. The remains of animals give clues to the kinds of vegetation which were found in an area, since certain animals thrive only on specific foods. Under suitable conditions, the types of vegetation can also be determined by a study of the deposits of peat, coal, and fossils embedded in rocks. The kinds of vegetation will usually indicate the type of climate which prevailed at that period of time.

Fragments of pottery, pieces of glass, portions of jewelry, discarded metal objects, and rusty weapons are also very useful in piecing together the life of the people who lived in the Scriptures. Written records engraved on stone, papyrus, pottery, goat skin, or clay tablets reveal a great deal about contemporary events. Buried receipts, treaties, records, letters, maps, and art all add to our knowledge of social customs and make the biblical peoples seem more real and alive.

Deposits of coins are very important factors in determining the dates of empires, kings, and historical occurrences. In Palestine, for example, Persian coins have been found which had been brought there at the close of the Babylonian Captivity in 536 B.C. The returning Hebrews acquired these coins during their 70-year sojourn in Babylon and continued to use them when they returned to Palestine to rebuild Jerusalem and its environs. Coins have been found from the period of Herod the Great (37-4 B.C.). Many have been discovered from the reign of Augustus (6-14 A.D.), Tiberius (14-37 A.D.), Claudius (37-54 A.D.), and Nero (54-56 A.D.). All of these help us to determine just when the biblical events took place. It was probably the silver denarius of Tiberius Caesar which Jesus held in his hand when the Herodians tried to entrap him in their tax problems (Matt. 22:19-22).

Other materials for the study of the origins of Judaism and of Christianity have come from the tombs and graves which have been preserved for posterity. Some of these tombs were literally "gold mines" for the archeologist and for those concerned with verifying the story of God's people. Many of these tombs contained great depositories of pottery, utensils, coins, furniture, seeds, foods, and clothing which threw considerable light on past cultures referred to in the Scriptures. Many of the inscriptions, mosaics, paintings, and carvings portray the influence which the Greeks, Romans, Egyptians, Babylonians, Assyrians, and other neighbors had upon the people of the Holy Land.

Inscriptions in tombs and upon the sarcophagi in which the bodies of the dead were placed serve as important sources of information to verify dates, people, and events of biblical times. These inscriptions often supply valuable information about laws and customs which would otherwise have been lost to posterity. Larger tombs had many rooms and halls lined with shelves, on which were stored urns containing the bones of departed loved ones. The Hebrews were always cramped for space in tiny Palestine and needed more room to bury their dead. Often they would take the bones from the decomposed remains of former interments from the burial bier and place them in urns, or ossuaries as they were sometimes called. These urns were often decorated with interesting designs, beautiful inlays, or mosaic work. The names of the deceased were often engraved upon the urns. Such names as Jesus, Simon, Judas, Mary, Elizabeth, Ananias, and Annas have been found; this indicates that they were common names in the Bible times. Some urns were marked with crosses, indicating that the departed were Christians.

Probably the greatest discovery of recent archeological history was that of Dr. Howard Carter. In 1923 he discovered the tomb of the youthful Pharaoh of Egypt, King Tutankhamen, who reigned in the 14th century B.C.[3] To the public, this was a sensational news item proclaimed in newspapers all over the world. The discovery of King Tutankhamen's tomb, filled as it was with an incredible variety of riches, popularized archeology as nothing had done before. Finds as productive as this, however, are rare. In most cases, the story of man's past is built up from tiny scattered remnants.

Some of the most valuable records of the past have been preserved in inscriptions and written documents. In Christian history especially, the most important finds have been the ancient manuscripts. These have taken several forms.

The earliest known manuscripts are written on papyrus, which came into use early in history. A tiny statue of an Egyptian scribe holding a roll of papyrus has been discovered and identified as having been made in Egypt about 2700 B.C. During the succeeding centuries papyrus came into common usage and spread to other lands. The dry climate of the Bible lands has been conducive to the preservation of this type of writing material. The oldest piece of papyrus found so far has been dated about 2300 B.C.

Papyrus was prepared from a reed that flourished along the banks of the Nile River in Egypt. The pith or pulp of this papyrus was sliced into very thin strips which were then laid horizontally, all in the same direction. Another layer was added at right angles, and the two layers were pressed together into a single sheet and dried. These sheets were then glued together at their edges to form a continuous roll 15 or more feet in length. The writer used pens made from reeds which had been thoroughly dried and sharpened, and a colored ink.

The usual form of a book made from papyrus was, of course, the scroll. In other words, the papyrus was simply rolled up around a stick. In Greek the whole scroll was usually called a "biblion" (meaning "book"); the plural is "biblia." The books of both the Old and New Testament were first written in scroll form and were hence called "biblia." From this the word Bible has come to us.

Such scrolls were very difficult to handle while reading; often, to find a specific passage, the scroll had to be completely unrolled. This scroll form eventually became just too unwieldy, so finally the sheets of papyrus began to be sewn together into pamphlet or book form. This new form, called a "codex," came into use in the second century B.C. and was used extensively by the early Christian writers.

The earliest New Testament codex so far discovered is a small portion of the Gospel of John, measuring about three and a half inches by two and a quarter inches. This tiny fragment has been dated in the first half of the second century. The oldest copy of a codex containing some of the epistles of Paul was discovered by Egyptian peasants in 1931. They found 11 codices which included portions of the Old Testament and a few of Paul's letters. These codices have been dated about 200 A.D., or about 150 years after Paul actually wrote his epistles.[4]

In the earliest Christian era, the manuscripts were written without any punctuation marks or breaks between the words. These so-called "cursive" or "running-together" codices looked something like this: "forgodso lovedtheworldthathegavehisonlysonthatwhoeverbelieves inhimshouldnotperishbuthaveeternallife." In this form of writing, the pen did not have to be lifted from the papyrus sheet. This increased the speed of writing, but at the same time it made the codex difficult to read and increased the possibilities for errors when scribes recopied the manuscripts. The vast majority of the New Testament writings were at first recorded in "cursive" form.

A second form of writing used in the early Christian era was called "uncial" because the capital letters used were about an inch in height. To form these capital letters required a great deal of painstaking skill. A codex in uncial form would look like this: "FORGODSOLOVED THEWORLDTHATHEGAVEHISONLYBEGOTTEN SONTHATWHOEVERBELIEVESINHIMSHOULD NOTPERISHBUTHAVEETERNALLIFE." This kind of manuscript proved too laborious and tedious to write. During the ninth century the modern form of writing began to supersede both the cursive and the uncial scripts.

Paul apparently dictated most of his epistles. However, he often added a closing sentence or two in his own hand-writing, which he described to the Galatians as being written with "large letters" (Gal. 6:11). We may infer from this that Paul's writing was probably stiff and angu-lar in form compared to the flowing script of the cursive letters usually used in documents written at the time.

Archeological findings have revealed that letters in Bible times were written in a form quite different from our letters today. The signature of the author, for exam-ple, was always placed at the beginning of the letter. On a scroll this was important, for the recipient would not need to unroll the entire missive in order to see whom the message was from.

This form of letter writing was much more practical than that of our own day. Who reads a letter until he has determined the author? Knowing the author gives a new meaning to any letter. Samples of letters discovered by archeologists in Egypt and the Holy Land take this form: "Theron to Heraclides, his brother, many greet-ings and wishes for good health . . . etc." "Tays to the Lord Apollonius, many greetings. Above all I greet you master, and am praying always for your health . . . etc." "Antonis Longus to Nils, his mother, many greetings. Continually I pray for your health . . . etc."

This historical knowledge clarifies for us why Paul's signature always comes at the beginning of each of his epistles in the New Testament. It also explains why near-ly every epistle in the New Testament begins with a greet-ing and a concern for the receiver of the letter. The au-thors of the epistles were simply using the accepted form of letter writing in their day.

During the past centuries archeology has been an active and fascinating study which has unraveled the history of the Bible by digging up the cities, sites, and remains of the Holy Land and its neighbors. The significance of biblical archeology is beyond dispute, for it has become a vital part of biblical research which has deepened our appreciation and understanding of the Scriptures. Biblical archeology has provided the general background for the history of God's people. Thanks to archeology, we now know a great deal more about the food, clothing, homes, and implements of the era from Abraham to Paul than is contained in the Bible alone. Archeology has helped to fill in the gaps of Bible history and to verify many events of the Scriptures. Many obscure passages in the Bible have been made more meaningful by a study of the civilizations unearthed in Palestine. Finally, the discoveries of the archeologists have helped to verify the trustworthiness of the biblical account. W. F. Albright writes, "There can be no doubt that archeology has confirmed the substantial historicity of the Old Testament." [5]

CHAPTER TWO

The Techniques
of Archeology

A century ago, such familiar biblical cities as Ur, Nineveh, Babylon, Jericho, and Samaria were just mounds of
rubble lost to posterity. In some cases, even the location
of these cities had been forgotten. Skeptics doubted the
details of the capture of Jericho, the ivory palaces of
Ahab at Samaria, the glories of ancient Babylon, the
stables of King Solomon, the customs of the Hebrews,
and many of the traditions written in the scriptural record. During the past hundred years, however, many
cities have been excavated, and evidence from the sites
often confirms details of the stories of the Scriptures.
The Old and New Testaments have acquired fresh meaning through scientific study by the archeologist.

Archeology, though, is a fairly young science; almost
all of our new knowledge has come to light only in the
last 100 years. From crude beginnings, archeology in the
last century has come to be an exact, meticulous, and specialized discipline.

This can be seen by looking at how much the techniques and approaches of archeology have evolved since its inception as a science.

At first, archeology was concerned with only surface exploration—little or no digging was involved. Only those artifacts which could be picked up from the surface of the soil were studied. This type of archeology was started in a systematic way in about 1830. Later, in about 1890, subsurface explorations were begun. An adequate staff was used, and a systematic study of the discoveries were made. An intricate study of pottery during this period made it possible to date the sites. This early period of subsurface archeology continued until World War I.

Beginning in the 1920's, the interest of archeologists was in so-called "comparative archeology," where discoveries from a Palestinian site were compared with those from other sites in Egypt, Babylon, Assyria, and Persia so as to ascertain dates, rules, nations, and civilizations involved in habitation of the sites.

More recently, since about 1948, control of the expeditions has been given over to the nations in which the sites are found. Indigenous teams do most of the actual work; outsiders are welcomed mainly as consultants, advisors, or scholars. Museums have been built in Egypt, Palestine, and other Bible lands to house new discoveries.

A modern archeological expedition must be a carefully planned scientific study. Permission to excavate must be obtained from the government of the land where the work is to take place. Each nation has its own specific requirements as to how the work should be accomplished, what is to be done with the discoveries, and where the artifacts are to be stored. Government permits are issued only to competent archeologists and recognized sponsoring organizations.

The staff of the archeological expedition consists of

a director, several assistants, an architect, a photographer, a pottery expert, and as many workers as the expedition can afford. It is usually wise to hire as many native workers as possible to do the actual digging. This avoids suspicion and enmity from local residents. These workers must be supervised by the trained archeologists of the staff.

The first step of the archeologist is to secure permission from the owners of the land to dig on their property. Then a survey map is made, so that the whole area to be excavated can be carefully laid out in squares which are numbered and marked. Pegs are set in the corners of each plot and marked with a string so that as artifacts are found, an accurate record may be kept of the exact location of each object in the tell.

Once digging is begun, the earth covering the site is carefully removed and dumped in a refuse heap. The workmen are divided into gangs with a foreman, pickmen, basket fillers, and carriers. Twice as many basket fillers as pickmen are needed, since they study and sift the shovelfuls of soil removed by the pickmen; great care must be taken to observe every particle of soil taken from the dig. No stone is removed until it can be determined that it is not part of a wall or foundation. Every artifact found in the soil is photographed before it is removed from the site. Pottery is placed in baskets. All coins are labeled. Every article is numbered, tagged, and marked as to its actual location in the grid. All data must be carefully recorded; every artifact must be drawn to scale and registered in duplicate under serial numbers. Each level is carefully photographed, numbered, and recreated so explicitly that an exact model can be made of each grid in the excavation.

The digging continues until a definite floor or area of human occupation has been discovered. This can be determined by the discovery of a bone, a piece of pottery, a wall, a foundation, a coin, or debris. The floor of a prehistoric hut may be very messy; debris, broken pottery, lost ornaments or weapons have often been trodden into the dirt floor. The mosaic floor of a Roman house, on the other hand, would probably be clean and free from litter. The occupants of such a civilization would probably have a rubbish heap nearby where they discarded their broken pottery, ornaments, and trash. These heaps would reveal a great deal about the culture of the inhabitants.

In excavating a site, the contents of each level will depend upon the final fate of the city, home, or hut. If the site had been abandoned, the inhabitants would probably have taken with them all of their important possessions, so that exploration would probably not be too rewarding. If the place had been destroyed by war, fire, earthquake, or some other catastrophe, however, debris from the destroyed structure and the furnishings of the place at the time of its destruction would be tumbled together in a potentially rewarding mess.

Above each level of civilization, or above each historical period, will be a layer of humus, dust, sand, and vegetation, depending on the climate and geographical location of the site. These layers will not contain much of archeological value since no people inhabited the area during this period of decay and disintegration.

The stratification of a site is often disturbed by later occupants who have dug into the old city to lay a foundation for their new home, or perhaps by a farmer who dug a pit to bury an animal or a cistern for his water supply. Such disturbances may introduce objects of a later period into the level of an ancient structure. Unless this foundation pit or disturbance is identified, it may confuse the evidence.

A frequent cause of disturbance in a level may have occurred when the next tenant removed stones of the former city to use in his own home. The walls of an abandoned structure could easily be dismantled and re-used, but such dismantling was usually done only to ground level. In such cases, the archeologist can often recover the lines of the foundation, since the floor levels would be intact.

Each layer of a site can be dated only by the ob-jects discovered in that stratum. It is therefore important to determine the layer in which an object is found and whether or not the layer was ever tampered with. If a layer contains an inscription of some kind, or a dated coin, or some distinctive architectural feature, the age of the stratum can easily be determined. The depth of an object has no value in itself unless it can be connect-ed with a definite layer of soil and a definite dating.

In most types of soil the layers can be observed through the mound. A new layer is indicated by a change in the texture of the soil or a change in its consistency or color. As soon as there is an indication of a new type of soil, the entire opening is usually cleared all the way down to this new level, so that the objects in the upper level will be kept separate from the lower one. If there is any doubt as to whether an object comes from the upper or lower level, it is usually assigned to the upper one, as it will cause less confusion in the layer already discovered than it will in the older stratum.

The materials discovered in an archeological site must be handled very carefully. Newly unearthed pottery, coins, or other artifacts are fragile, especially when first uncovered. The soil must not be rubbed off, for doing so may mar or scratch the surface. The earth's coating is also a good guide as to whether the artifacts have come from the same layer. Wooden articles are always rotted.

In some cases, liquid plastic is poured into the decayed portions of wood, so that when the plastic has dried, the resultant form can be reconstructed from the hardened plastic which fills the openings left by decay and rot. Clay tablets, softened by moisture during their long burial, must be carefully rebaked before any attempt is made to clean and study them. The fragile bones of human and animal skeletons have to be treated with wax so that they can be removed just as they were found in the dig. Muslin reinforcements prove to be a real help in holding mosaic pieces together while they are being moved to storage areas. Papier-mâché can be used to take the imprint of inscriptions on obelisks, tombs, and monuments. Liquid latex rubber will also give a clear imprint, making it possible to study the inscriptions in the comfort of a laboratory.

It is always best to complete the work on one layer before digging into the next, so that there will not be too large an accumulation of unclassified artifacts at the end of the excavation. The washing procedure should be done simply. The tray of soiled artifacts should be placed near the pans of water and the receiving tray for the cleaned pottery should be on the other side. Labeling should be done as soon as possible to avoid slip-ups in identification. Artifacts should be washed one at a time, so that there will be no injury and so that nothing be left behind in the silt remaining at the bottom of the washing basin. When the artifacts are thoroughly dry, they should be packed in cases and put away for storage and further study.

Some artifacts need special care even before they are lifted from the tell. Many objects are so fragile that there is a danger that they may be injured when they are removed from the soil. Paraffin wax has often been used to strengthen these fragile objects. The wax, however, often penetrates the object and makes further study difficult. Recently, a plastic emulsion has been used to protect the more delicate finds. In many cases a whole block of earth is removed together with the artifact, and in this way more time can be given to its protection and strengthening.

Written reports are carefully made of the finds in each layer or stratum as soon as possible, so that no information is forgotten. Often a large archeological staff will include a full-time recorder who will also make drawings of the various finds and artifacts.

It is not just the excavator digging into the earth who discovers the secrets of the past. Often a cameraman flying high above the Bible lands can determine much of the layout of a city, fortification, or site. Because of the proper ties of the earth's surface, pictures taken from the air can give a clearer representation than a study on the ground level. When soil has been disturbed, it seldom settles to the same compactness as the undisturbed soil around it. A lost cistern, storage pit, or basement fills up with sand, dust, and debris in the natural process of disuse. After many years it becomes a level field. The soil in the open pit is always lighter in texture, holds more moisture, and produces a more luxuriant growth. This can readily be detected by flying above the area before the field is harvested.

Shallow soil, on the other hand, hinders growth, resists moisture, and cramps roots. Air photography can reveal old road beds, walls, and foundations where grain appears to be stunted, parched, or discolored. What the camera reveals about the ground plan, design, and outlines of a site, the archeologist can later examine in detail with his spade.

The first important question an archeologist will ask about an artifact is "How old is it?" Here atomic science has proved valuable. It is known that all living organisms, human beings, animals, trees, and plants absorb carbon dioxide from the air and take in, with the carbon dioxide, minute quantities of a radio-active form of carbon known now as carbon 14. Since all animals depend upon plants for their food, it means that all animal bodies contain carbon 14. When an animal dies, however, it takes in no more carbon 14. Instead, its radioactive carbon begins to decay at a rate which has been precisely measured. In dead bodies, the ratio of carbon 14 to nonradioactive carbon decreases at a fixed rate. After 5568 years, half of the carbon 14 content is lost. In the next 5568 years, half of the remaining carbon 14 disappears, etc. By comparing the amount of carbon 14 left in a dead body with the amount it had when alive, a scientist can determine the date when the organism died. This means of determining the amount of radioactive carbon in a dead body can be used to determine the age of trees, shells, charcoal, indeed of any once living thing. Thus, carbon 14 has proved to be very helpful to archeologists who wish to date the ancient and pre-Christian periods of history.

Archeology has opened the vistas of the past and brought to light civilizations which had lain sleeping for thousands of years. Systematic explorations of the tells which dot the "fertile crescent" have verified the historical authenticity of the Scriptures and given many rich insights into the customs, cultures, and commerce of the Bible Land people. The use of highly specialized techniques and the cooperative efforts of competently trained archeologists have pieced together much of the intricate mosaic of the past into a panorama of certainty and clarity. As a result of the skill of these archeologists, the Bible reader today can have a clearer picture of God's chosen people.

CHAPTER THREE

The Patriarchs

What does archeology have to tell us about Abraham, Isaac, Jacob, and Joseph? No written records dealing with the patriarchs have ever been found outside of the Scriptures, but archeology has still made many discoveries which give a fascinating insight into the lives of these founding fathers of the Hebrew religion. As a result of the years of effort, we know quite a lot about the patriarch peoples, the way they lived, what they believed, the neighbors they lived with, and the culture of their times.

We know first of all that the patriarchs, like the Arabs, Babylonians, and Phoenicians, came from a so-called "Semitic" people who originated in western Asia. They were all described in Genesis as descendants of Shem, the son of Noah, and were thus given the name Semites. The patriarchs were wandering nomads (see for example, Deut. 26:5) in a part of the world which was not too productive or fruitful, yet they and their descendants became leaders of the world in philosophy, science, culture, and business. The beginnings of these great

Hebrews were humble and simple, yet they have left a greater impact on the Western world than Egypt, Assyria, Babylon, or Persia. Their culture has permeated deeper than that of the Greeks and the Romans.

The patriarchs were also called Hebrews, which probably comes from a word meaning "from the other side of [the river]"; hence a foreigner. The word "Hebrew" may also refer to an expression used in Gen. 10:21, "To Shem also the father of all the children of Eber." Usually when the term Hebrew was applied to the Israelites, the speaker was a foreigner (Gen. 39:14, 17; Gen. 41:12; Ex. 1:16; Ex. 2:6). When the patriarchs referred to themselves as "Hebrews," it was only when they were speaking to foreigners (Gen. 40:15; Ex. 1:19; Jonah 1:9).

The patriarchs were so named because they were organized into a unique form of social organization according to families. In this "patriarchal" system, the father was the supreme ruler of the entire clan, including the grandchildren and the great-grandchildren. He had the authority to put any member of his tribe to death if necessary. The patriarch furnished the home for the entire family; all the earnings of his sons went into his coffers. All of the produce of the fields were gathered into a common storage bin. All of the women went into the fields to help with the patriarch's harvest.

Marriage was extremely significant. Each son brought home a wife to live in the family tent or house, but the daughters married men from other clans and went to live with their husband's father, increasing the strength of the neighboring tribe by adding another worker. As a result, daughters were not nearly as desirable as sons. Each son added to the protection and prosperity of his father's household; hence it was a deep concern of every father to have many sons. The family clan must be strengthened and defended! For a woman to be childless was a disgrace and humiliation, since she offered nothing to the family strength. An heir was absolutely essential; if a husband died childless, it was necessary for his widow to marry her husband's brother in order that there might be an heir to carry on the family traditions. Hence, the Sadducees told the story of a woman who married seven brothers, but in each case there were no heirs (Mark 12:18-23). In such a case, at the death of the father it would be necessary for the oldest son to become the patriarch.

Abraham

According to the Genesis account, Abraham, the first of the patriarchs, was born in about 1800 B.C. at Ur, about 100 miles from the Persian Gulf (Gen. 11:31). Abraham's line of descent came through Noah's son Shem (Gen. 11:10-32), but the genealogy of Abraham may not be complete; often only the important members of the family clan were listed. The word "father" has at least seven different shades of meaning in the Hebrew, while the term "son" has twelve distinct meanings, so that it is very difficult to determine the genealogy of many of the people listed in the Scriptures from the biblical record alone.

Ur, the first home of Abraham and his family, is today a barren, forbidding desert. Until archeologists began to work there, Ur was a lost city buried in sand-swept loneliness. But thanks to the discoveries of archeology, we now know that Ur was at one time a prosperous, fertile, and productive city supporting a great population. Archeological excavations, under the direction of Sir Leonard Woolley and others in 1922-34, have given us many new insights into the place where the patriarchal history begins.

It is now possible to reconstruct a positive picture of

life in Ur. The city was about four miles long and one and one-half miles wide. The streets, made only for foot traffic, were narrow and unpaved. An average dwelling in the city measured 40 by 52 feet. A middle-class family had from 10 to 20 rooms in its home. The lower walls were built of burned brick, while the upper portions were constructed of unbaked mud bricks. The entire wall was usually plastered and whitewashed. All of the rooms in the home opened into a central court. On the lower level, the kitchen, lavatory, and servants' quarters were located. The family chapel or worship center was usually at the back of the house. The family rooms were on the second floor.[1]

In the excavations at Ur a school was discovered. Many clay writing tablets were unearthed where one side was written upon by the student and the other side inscribed by the teacher. The writing was in cuneiform signs made on flattened slabs of softened clay. Education included the three "R's"—reading, writing, and arithmetic. Several clay tablets indicate that students first learned to solve problems in square and cube roots. On some tablets, the teacher had inscribed a list of words with their phonetic values, syllables, and symbols which the pupil reproduced on the reverse side. Other tablets indicate the declension of nouns and verbs in use at this time.[2]

Archeological studies at Ur have revealed the type of religion which was prevalent at the time. The chief god was Nannar, the moon god. His "ziggurat," or temple, was a gigantic structure in the midst of the city; it was 1200 feet in length and 600 feet in width and rose to a height of about 75 feet. It was constructed of solid brick using burnt bricks as the exterior covering.

A single flight of 100 steps led to the top of the edifice. Gifts offered to the gods were kept in the huge store rooms of the ziggurat.

The temple staff included priests, supervisors of the harem, and ministers of war, agriculture, transportation, and finance. Some of the gifts brought for sacrificial purposes were cattle, sheep, barley, cheese, butterfat, and wool. Other evidence indicates that each family had a niche in its home reserved for a statue or idol used in family worship.[3]

It was this type of culture and civilization that Abraham and his family left to go to Haran in Mesopotamia (present-day Syria) to live. The new home was called "the field of Aram" or "Aram of the Two Rivers," since it was located between the Tigris and Euphrates Rivers. Abraham's descendants, who remained in Haran, were called "Arameans" or "Men of Aram" (Gen. 28:5, 31:20, 24). As the chief city of this area, Haran was mentioned frequently in contemporary letters and documents. Cuneiform tablets indicate that it was a thriving and flourishing commercial center of that day.

Excavations at Mari, near Haran, have uncovered one of the most fabulous palaces of all time. The palace covered over 15 acres and contained nearly 300 rooms. In the library, 20,000 clay tablets were discovered. These are called the Mari tablets; some of these indicate that Mesopotamia was often involved in biblical events. A number of names from the eleventh chapter of Genesis have been found in the Mari Tablets.[4]

The Nuzi Tablets

A number of years ago archeologists uncovered the archives of Nuzi, a city about 300 miles southeast of Haran. The tablets found in this library date from the 15th and 14th centuries B.C. They provide a striking picture of the customs and traditions of Mesopotamia which influenced the life of Abraham at Haran. They also clarify a number of customs referred to in Genesis which formerly were very obscure. In Genesis 15:3, for example, Abraham complains to God, "Behold, thou hast given me no offspring; and a slave born in my house will be my heir." Eliezer, a trusted servant, who had charge of all that Abraham owned, was selected to be his heir. Why should an outsider be selected for this important post? The Nuzi Tablets helped to explain this. It was the custom for an heirless family in Mesopotamia to adopt someone as a son; the one chosen would care for the husband and wife, provide for their welfare, and insure them an honorable burial. In return for his services, the adopted heir was to inherit the estate. In case a son was born to the family later, the agreement was nullified. Thus, at one time, Eliezer was heir apparent to the estate of Abraham, but the birth of Isaac ended the high position. Because of this need for an heir, Sarah, as well as Leah and Rachel, suggested to their husbands that they have a child by their maids to provide an heir for the family.[5]

Abraham in Canaan

While living in Haran of Mesopotamia, Abraham was called by God in a unique way to go down into Canaan (modern Palestine) to live. There Abraham's family was to become a special nation, with a special blessing, and a special promise (Gen. 12:1-3). When Abraham came to Canaan, he stopped first at Moreh (Gen. 12:6), in southern Palestine. It was at Moreh that Abraham traditionally built the first altar to the Lord ever erected in the Holy Land (Gen. 12:7). Later he moved his tent, belongings, and wife a few miles to the south, settling between Bethel and Ai (Gen. 12:8), about 12 miles north of Jerusalem; at Bethel, Abraham built a second altar to the Lord. Nearly all of the towns associated with Abraham have now been excavated and identified; it is now quite evident that Shechem, Bethel, and Ai were cities in existence at Abraham's time. Even the name "Abraham" has been found on the clay tablets discovered in the area of these three cities.

Abraham in Egypt

A famine forced Abraham and his family to leave Canaan and to go down into Egypt where the floods of the Nile River assured a crop every year. Archeological discoveries in Egypt show that strangers from the region of Palestine and Syria did travel into Egypt at the time of Abraham's exodus. A painting in a tomb at Beni-Hassan, dated about 2000 B.C., indicated that Semites were in Egypt at this time.[6]

Once again, the knowledge gained through archeology has been useful in clarifying an obscure portion of Scripture. A papyrus document has been found which tells about an incident in which the Pharaoh took a beautiful woman from her husband, putting him to death and bringing her into his court. It is easy to see why Abraham in Egypt wanted it to be known that Sarah was his sister (Gen. 12:11-13). In fact, Abraham was not guilty of a falsehood, since Sarah was actually his sister (Gen. 20:12).

The Scriptures list many of the things which Abraham took with him into Egypt: "And he had sheep, and oxen, and he-asses, and menservants, and maidservants, and she-asses, and camels" (Gen. 12:16). Archeological monuments discovered in Egypt indicate the presence of such animals in use at the time of Abraham. Pictures of these animals were carved on the walls of the temple erected to Queen Hatshepsut in 1504-1452 B.C., and on other tombs in Egypt. Even statuettes and figurines of

these animals have been found in Egypt which date from
a period as early as 3000 B.C.[7]

Abraham Returns to Canaan

When Abraham returned to Palestine after his sojourn
in Egypt, the Bible story tells us, he discovered that there
was friction and strife between his herdsmen and those
of his nephew Lot. Abraham suggested they separate; he
offered Lot any site which he might choose. Lot chose
the fertile and well-watered plains of the Jordan Valley
(Gen. 13:11). Today this whole area is the hottest and
most desolate part of Palestine. Temperatures often run
from 105 degrees to 120 degrees. The land is parched
and barren. Certainly Lot would not have chosen such
a site for his flocks. Nelson Glueck's exploration of this
area in 1940, though, indicated that the land along the
Jordan and the Dead Sea must have been densely inhabited at one time. Dr. Glueck has discovered the sites
of 70 ancient cities, some of them more than 5000 years
old. Archeology has revealed that Lot chose the best land
for himself.[8]

God's Covenant with Abraham

In his covenant with Abraham, God promised that he
would bless Abraham so that he would become a blessing to those about him, that all of the world would be
blessed by Abraham's family (Gen. 12:1-3). Abraham
would possess the promised land, and his posterity would
be as numerous as the "stars of the heavens" (Gen. 22:17),
"the dust of the earth" (Gen. 13:16), and the "sands of
the sea" (Gen. 32:12).

This covenant proved to be a real concern to Abraham, for he and Sarah did not have any children. The

Nuzi Tablets included several laws regarding marriage and children. One law indicated the purpose of marriage was to have an heir for the family.[9] Another law was included which permitted the wife to give her servant to her husband in order that there might be an heir. If a wife did not have a son, she could be forced by a clause in her marriage contract to supply her husband with another wife. The wife's position could be protected by keeping such a woman in servitude. Hence Sarah gave Abraham her handmaid, Hagar, so that she might bear an heir—thus Hagar bore a son, Ishmael. In this case Abraham and Sarah were simply following the laws and directives of the land from which they came.

The Cave of Machpelah

Sarah is the only woman in the Bible whose age is given, probably because she was the mother of the "chosen race." After her death at 127, Abraham wanted to buy the cave of Machpelah at Hebron, which was located about 20 miles south of Jerusalem, as a family burial plot. The lot, which included the cave of Machpelah, belonged to a Hittite named Ephron. According to the Hittite codes, taxes on real estate were paid by the original owner so long as he held on to any part of the property. Abraham, to avoid paying this levy, wanted to buy only the cave, but Ephron insisted on selling the land as well as the cave so that Abraham would be required by law to pay the tax. Since Sarah had to be buried on the day of death, Abraham was in no condition to bargain; he was forced to buy the whole field in order to secure the cave. Thus Abraham had to pay the tax also.

When Abraham paid for the cave, he weighed out 400 shekels of silver (Gen. 23:16). This indicates that money was measured by weight instead of coins at that time. Archeological discoveries reveal that coinage of silver and gold in the Bible lands did not begin until about 700 B.C. Thus, the shekel was a weight rather than a coin in the days of the patriarchs. Today a Moslem mosque stands over the patriarchal burial chamber. No one has been able to visit the cave to see if anything remains from ancient times.

Isaac

When Abraham wanted a wife for his son he sent his faithful and trusted servant Eliezer back to Nahor in Mesopotamia to find a wife among his own relatives. In a caravan of ten camels and an adequate entourage, Eliezer went to Nahor. At the well there he met Rebekah, who took him to the house of her father, Bethuel, a nephew of Abraham (Gen. 24:10-14). Rebekah consented to go with Eliezer to Canaan, where she would marry a relative she had never seen.

Isaac took Rebekah to be his wife and went to live in Gerar in the country of the Philistines. There God gave to Isaac the same promise made to Abraham, that of blessings, land, family, and prosperity (Gen. 26:1-5). While in Gerar, Isaac, like his father, told the natives that his wife was his sister. The custom still prevailed whereby the king could choose any woman he wanted to be his wife. Isaac knew the law, and he feared that the beauty and dignity of Rebekah might prove his downfall, so he deceived the natives of Gerar.

Isaac's Blessing

When Isaac was well along in years he decided to bestow his blessing upon Esau, his first-born son (Gen. 27:1-10). Rebekah, however, wanted to have the blessing given to her favorite son Jacob, so she formulated a plan to deceive her aged husband. When Isaac discovered he had blessed the wrong son, he was filled with remorse, but he did not revoke his oral blessing, since it was considered sacred and irrevocable.

Archeology has thrown considerable light on the validity of these oral blessings. In fact, evidence from the Nuzi Tablets also indicate that oriental people often sold their birthright for sheep, cattle, or jewelry. Thus Esau's selling of his birthright was a common custom according to Mesopotamian practices, and not contrary to law. The inheritance rights were at this time negotiable from brother to brother.[10]

Jacob

Jacob was forced by Esau's anger to leave home after he had stolen the blessing of their father Isaac. Rebekah encouraged Jacob to flee, for if Esau killed Jacob, then the family clan in turn would have to kill Esau, and Rebekah would lose both of her sons (Gen. 27:41-45).

Jacob went to his mother's home in Nahor of Mesopotamia. Here he stayed for 20 years, working seven years for Leah, seven years for Rachel, and six years for his flocks and herds (Gen. 29:15-35). Such a contract, through which a man pays by labor for his wife, has been found among the Nuzi Tablets.[11]

Jacob sensed jealousy arising between him and his father-in-law, so he decided to return to Palestine. While packing to move, his wife Rachel stole the family "gods" or images. When the discovery was made, her father Laban came in great haste, pursuing Jacob for seven days until he caught up with the caravan in the hill country at Gilead. Laban was incensed that Jacob had left without telling him, and he was furious at the discovery that the family idols had been taken (Gen. 31:25).

According to the Nuzi Tablets the family idols were very significant gods; they had to be kept in the family to guarantee prosperity and the right of inheritance. One of the tablets says that if a son-in-law gained possession of the family images, he could appear in court and make a claim to the estate of the father-in-law.

Laban, then, knew that if Jacob possessed the family gods, he could some day claim the right to his father-in-law's estate. It is little wonder that Laban hurried after Jacob. This also explains why Rachel so carefully hid them in her saddle bag. Only by the labors of archeologists could any of this have come to light.

Joseph

One day Joseph, as a lad of 17, was sent by his father Jacob to check on the well-being of his brothers, who were grazing the flocks in the pastures near Shechem. Joseph discovered that they had left Shechem and were pasturing flocks at a place called Dothan.

When Joseph's brothers saw him coming, they were prompted by jealousy to make plans to kill him. Reuben felt sorry for his brother, probably for his father's sake, and suggested that Joseph be thrown into a pit and kept alive. Palestine is filled with old cisterns, which were dug to water the flocks and to furnish the water supply for the tribes. Many of these were discarded when the towns were uprooted. Archeologists digging at Gezer have found a number of skeletons in the bottom of cisterns which indicates they were often used to hold prisoners.[12]

Joseph's life, of course, was spared; he was sold into slavery. This was a very common occurrence among the peoples of that time. Archeological discoveries in Egypt have uncovered many accounts showing that Hebrew slaves were highly prized. Important Egyptians felt that it increased their social status to have overseers in their house from other lands, so it was not strange that Potiphar should set Joseph over his household.

Later, when Joseph described his position in Egypt to his brothers, he referred to himself as "Father of Pharaoh; Lord of all his house, and ruler throughout the land of Egypt." Egyptian monuments indicate that Joseph was simply using common Egyptian titles. Such use indicates the familiarity of Joseph with the customs and practices of Egypt (Gen. 45:8). The titles "Chief of Butlers" and "Chief of Bakers" occur frequently in Egyptian inscriptions. The birthday of Pharaoh was known to have been an occasion for feasting; often prisoners were released during these birthday celebrations.

Joseph Moves to Egypt

When the brothers of Joseph brought their father to Egypt to live, Jacob appeared before Pharaoh and referred to his age as "few and evil," though 130 years would hardly be few. Egyptian sources, however, help us to remember that Jacob was here speaking to the Pharaoh of Egypt, who was regarded as an eternally living god; Jacob was only following court etiquette by belittling himself.

Jacob died after living for 17 years in Egypt. At his death, the brothers had his body mummified in the Egyptian manner. This elaborate preparation of the body for burial required 40 days (Gen. 50:3). Archeological records show that embalmers used a liberal supply of fine linen, spices, oils, and perfumes in their art. The heart, lungs, liver and intestines were removed and placed in four vessels called "canopic" jars. The body was soaked in natron (hydrated sodium carbonate) and then wrapped in many yards of linen. Between the layers of linen were placed a large quantity of spices, oils, and perfumes. The dry climate of Egypt also helped to preserve the mummies.

According to many current views of archeologists, the period of the patriarchs would include the years from 1800 to 1500 B.C. For the sake of convenience, it is helpful to remember that the date for Abraham's life would be 1800 B.C. This was a significant period in the history of God's chosen people, for the patriarchy established many of the backgrounds and customs which still prevail today among the Jewish people.

CHAPTER FOUR

The Exodus from Egypt

The Exodus from Egypt was one of the turning-point experiences in the history of the Hebrews. They became increasingly convinced that in this unique event God had revealed himself in a special way to his people and had begun to form the Israelites in Egypt into the core of a nation which would become so strong that it would never disappear from history. The happenings in Egypt, the desert, the wanderings in the wilderness gave the Hebrews an unshakable conviction of God's great power and might. God was the "One" who could make both nature and the hardened heart of Pharaoh serve his purposes, yet he was a God of love and mercy. The servitude in Egypt and the wanderings in the wilderness changed the whole pattern of Hebrew thought and life and brought into being a people through whom God would bless the whole world.

The Israelites in Goshen

The quiet, settled life of the patriarchal families in Palestine came to an end when a famine in Israel forced Jacob to send his sons to Egypt for food. The dreams of

Joseph were fulfilled as his brothers bowed down to him in their request to buy grain. Joseph could not keep his identity secret for long; he let his brothers know who he was and asked them to bring his father to him. The family of Jacob at that time numbered 70 souls (Gen. 46:27); if we include Joseph's family, the total number of Hebrews living in Egypt would be about 75—a small beginning.

According to the biblical account Pharaoh suggested that Joseph give the land of Goshen to his brothers and their families. Goshen was on the eastern part of the Nile delta, one of the richest parts of Egypt. Edward Robinson, the first Palestinian archeologist, reported that in 1839 the land of Goshen yielded more revenue than any other province of Egypt. He continues by saying there were more herds and flocks here than anywhere else. Archeologists have discovered that some of the cities in Goshen were named Succoth, Zephon, Migdol, Silu, and very likely Goshen itself; these words are Hebrew in origin, indicating that the Jews had lived here at one time.

The Hyksos

Archeologists have shown that at about the time that Joseph and his family came into Egypt (c. 1700 B.C.) the Hyksos, an Asiatic race of people, had infiltrated Egypt. By c. 1730 they had gained control of the Nile valley, forming two Hyksos dynasties which ruled until 1570 B.C. The Egyptians hated and feared these foreigners who had built a great empire out of their land. Since the Hebrews and the Hyksos were both from Semitic and Canaanite stock, it is easy to see why Joseph and his family were treated so well during the period of Hyksos domination.[1] Millar Burrows, an eminent archeologist, says, "Modern historians agree, on the whole, that the conditions of the Hyksos period offered a natural setting for Joseph's rise to power and for the settlement of his family in Egypt." [2]

Archeological evidence also reveals that the Hyksos often used Hebrew names such as Hur and Yacob-hur.[3] The natural tie between the Hyksos rulers of Egypt and the rise of Joseph paved the way for Joseph to become ruler "over all the land of Egypt" (Gen. 41:43).

The Hyksos rulers controlled Egypt for 150 years. Excavations in Egypt indicate that Avaris, on the Nile delta, was the Hyksos capital. The tremendous Hyksos fortifications have been unearthed, revealing their great power and strength in Egypt.

Finally the Hyksos rulers in Egypt were forced out of power by insurgent Egyptians in about 1580 B.C. and driven back into Palestine. Naturally, the new rulers of Egypt would have an inborn fear of the Hebrews who had infiltrated their land; they could attempt to take over the government at any time, as the Hyksos had done.

Out of this new ruling power came the Pharaohs "who did not know Joseph." The new dynasty of Egyptian Pharaohs treated the Hebrews inhumanly. Joseph's descendants were forced to work on government projects involving the building of two great store-cities, Pithom and Raamses. The Israelites made the bricks for the building of these two cities by hand. To make their task even more oppressive, Pharaoh forced them to gather their own straw for making the bricks, though they were still required to turn out the same number of bricks. The Israelites complained, "behold your servants are beaten" (Ex. 5:16).

A beating was not so much a matter of brutality as it was a normal expression of the relation between men of unequal status in Egypt. Getting any work done in Egypt without a beating was rare. Under such conditions, they

were required to build the store-cities of Pithom and
Raamses⁴ (Ex. 1:11). The sites of both of the cities were
first located and excavated by Sir Flinders Petrie in 1905-
1906. Archeologists digging in these ruins at Pithom and
Raamses have made two interesting discoveries: these two
cities were used as storehouses for the treasures of Egypt.
and some of the bricks of the city seem to be made
without straw.

Moses

According to the Exodus account, the mother of Moses
refused to throw her newborn son into the waters of the
Nile. The Pharaoh's daughter, who found the baby boy,
named him Moses. An Egyptian princess would not be
likely to give her newly adopted boy a Hebrew name,
especially since the Hebrews were now of such ill repute
in Egypt. The name Moses, as a result, probably came
from an Egyptian word "Mose," which means "the
child," or the word "mes," which means "to bear or
beget." It is surprising how many Egyptian names are
included in the genealogies of the Levites, such as Moses,
Assir, Haphni, Phinehas, Puti-el, all of which are dis-
tinctly Egyptian in origin.

Moses in Midian

One day Moses came upon an Egyptian who attacked
an Israelite. This angered Moses so much that he inter-
vened and in the melee killed the Egyptian. Moses, realizing the seriousness of a Hebrew slaying an Egyptian,
fled to Midian, in the Arabian desert (Ex. 2:15), where
he spent 40 years tending the sheep of Jethro and learning the art of self-preservation in desert living. Here
Moses gained adequate preparation for the task to which
he would later be called; in no other way could Moses

have been trained to care for the Israelites who would some day flee Egypt and be forced to spend 40 years in the desert on the way to Palestine.

Moses' Call from God

As the well-known story relates, the call of God for Moses to begin his work came from a burning bush at the end of his 40 years in the desert of Midian. Moses objected to God's call by stating that the people would not listen to him and that he could not succeed because of his speech difficulty. God took care of the first objection by giving Moses the ability to perform miracles, and handled the second objection by appointing Aaron as the spokesman for his brother Moses.

Moses and Aaron went before Pharaoh with God's message: "Let my people go." This Pharaoh is usually referred to as the Pharaoh of the Exodus. If Seti I (1308-1290) was the Pharaoh of the Oppression, then his successor Rameses II (1290-1224) would be the Pharaoh whom Moses approached.[5] This Pharaoh, however, continually refused to release his Hebrew slaves. Even the signs Moses performed were not enough to convince him that God was with the Hebrews; his heart remained hardened (Ex. 4:21, 7:3, 9:12, etc.). Eventually Pharaoh's oppression proved too much to bear, and Moses and the Israelites fled.

Moses Leads His People from Egypt

After hundreds of years in Egypt, the Israelites were finally led by Moses on the long trip back into the Holy Land (Ex. 12:40, 41). During their stay in Egypt they had increased from 75 souls (Ex. 1:5) to a large nation.

It is interesting but not surprising to note that nothing

remains in the monuments or tablets of Egypt about the details of the sojourn of the Israelites. The Egyptians, however, always removed from their records anything that was derogatory, distasteful, or uncomplimentary to their national history. Every monument of the Hyksos, for example, was completely destroyed after their expulsion from the land. The Egyptians had an interesting way of eradicating everything from history which they wanted to forget.

The route of the Exodus led the Israelites eastward through the Egyptian delta, from Rameses to Succoth (Ex. 12:37), then to Etham (Ex. 13:20), and finally to Bael-Zephon by the shores of the Red Sea (Ex. 14:2). On this trackless route the Israelites would not be so easily followed; had they taken a northern route to Canaan, they would have faced the Philistines who were warlike and well equipped for battle. Moreover, this northern route to Canaan was a major highway, and it was well guarded by the Egyptians. The children of Israel needed to cross the Red Sea in order to escape the Egyptian fortresses which guarded the main route to Canaan; the trackless southern roadway was much safer.

Archeologist M. G. Kyle has observed that travelers following the coast of the Red Sea today along the line of the Exodus do not need any guide book except the Bible; the topography still corresponds closely to that suggested in the biblical narrative.[6]

After the miraculous crossing of the Red Sea (Ex. 14:21 ff.), the Israelites continued their journey into the wilderness of Shur (Ex. 15:22). The wilderness of Shur lay directly east of the gulf of Suez; here the Israelites encountered a terrifying and waterless desert which provided no means of escape from the famishing thirst of the burning sands. Soon murmurings of fear and discontent arose. Finally, the pilgrims came to the spring Marah, but the bitter waters were unpalatable until Moses made them sweet with a tree which he threw into the spring (Ex. 15:25). The exact location of Marah is not known; however, a site called Huware, which still has a basin of bitter water, might be the spring which refreshed the thirsty Israelites.[7]

The next stop of the pilgrims was at Elim with its 12 springs and 70 palm trees. This is thought to be the present-day Wadi Churundel, five miles from Huware (Marah). Wadi Churundel is an oasis fringed with palms, feathery tamarisks, and acacia trees.

The Wilderness of Sin, an extensive sandy plain, was the next stop for the Israelites (Ex. 16:1); here they were fed manna (Ex. 14:36). At the next stop, called Rephidim, Moses struck the rock to supply water to quench the craving thirst of God's people. Here also, God sustained the Israelites in the battle against the Amalekites while Hur and Aaron held up the hands of Moses as he raised the rod of God. (Ex. 17:8-13).

Mount Sinai

In the third month after the Israelites' departure from Egypt, they arrived at last at Mt. Sinai, where they remained for a year. Sinai is a triangular peninsula 260 miles long and 150 miles wide. The southern part of the peninsula is a great mass of granite mountains which rise to a height of 8000 feet above sea level. Here the traditional site of Sinai, where Moses received the tablets of the Law, has been placed. Others feel that Mt. Sinai might be located in Midian. However, it seems that the traditional site is more logical. It is today called Jebel Musa, and is about 7,375 feet high.[8] All of the experiences recounted from Exodus 19:1 through the entire book of Leviticus and as far as Numbers 10:12 traditionally are said to have taken place during this 12-month sojourn at Sinai.

Mt. Sinai is referred to by name 35 times in the Old Testament. Seventeen times this same mountain is referred to as Horeb; the two are evidently the same place. At the base of the mountain lies a large plain, which was probably the place where the Israelites camped for a year. According to the story, it was here that God gave his people the Ten Commandments and the religious, ceremonial, and civil laws which were to guide the Israelites until the prophecies of the coming Messiah were fulfilled.

Code of Hammurabi

Archeologists have uncovered many interesting codes of laws which were made and used by the Hittites, Assyrians, Babylonians, and Persians. As a result, many new insights have been gained about the civil, ceremonial, and religious laws of the Hebrews. The best example, the famous Code of Hammurabi was discovered in Susa, near the Persian Gulf, in 1901-1902. The Code is inscribed on a slab of black diorite stone seven feet tall and about six feet wide. The Code contains 247 laws, written in 3600 lines. These laws deal with the moral, social, commercial, and economic life of the Babylonians. At the top of the stone, Hammurabi, king of Babylon in about 1700 B.C., is shown receiving these laws from the sun god.

Hammurabi's Code throws a great deal of light upon the social and moral customs of the peoples of that time. The Code states, for example, that in Babylon a wife might give a servant as a secondary wife to her husband, in order that there might be an heir to the family fortunes. If a son struck his father, his hand should be cut off. If an eye was injured, the guilty person should lose his eye; the same held true of breaking a bone in some person's body. If anyone stole an ox, sheep, goat, or pig, he should restore it tenfold.[9] These and other laws are obviously very close to the Old Testament statutes.

Ras Shamra Tablets

Another fascinating discovery was the Ras Shamra Tablets, found in Syria in 1928. While plowing in a field, a peasant woman uncovered the site of an ancient city called Ugarit, founded 2000 B.C. It had been a flourishing city noted for its commerce and culture. In the ruins of the city was a library which housed hundreds of cuneiform tablets in eight or nine different languages. These tablets mention the Hebrews and many other ancient peoples.

The tablets are from an inch and a half to ten inches in height. Many sacrifices are described in these tablets. The people of Ugarit practiced wave offerings, tribute offerings, and the offerings of the first fruits, as did the Hebrews. The offerings had to be without blemish or spot. The boiling of a kid in its mother's milk was permitted in a ritual for producing rain; this was forbidden by the Hebrews (Ex. 23:19). There are many references to Baal, but on the whole the Ras Shamra Tablets have also shown us just how common and widespread were many of the Mosaic Laws.

The Israelites Approach the Promised Land

After Israel left Mt. Sinai, they were guided by the pillar of cloud by day and the pillar of fire by night to Kadish-barnea, about 40 miles from Beersheba in the southernmost part of Palestine. From there 12 spies were sent to survey the promised land. After a 40-day trip, the spies returned with stories of giants, walled cities, and luscious fruit. Of the 12, only Joshua and Caleb wanted to go in to conquer the land, but the people rejected their advice. Because of their unbelief, the Bible states, the Hebrews were punished by God with a 40-year imprisonment in the wilderness. Most of these long, lonely years were spent at Kadish-barnea.

Not until all of the Israelites who were above 20 years of age at the time of the Exodus were dead did the people finally leave for the last lap of this journey into Canaan (Num. 14:20-35). When they came to Edom, their Edomite cousins refused to give them permission to pass through their country. (The Edomites were the descendants of Esau.) The Hebrews were forced to go around Edom, then north to the plains of Moab, where they encountered Balaam, the prophet. After Balaam's dealings with the Israelites, the people finally crossed the plains of Moab and came to the north end of the Dead Sea (Num. 22:1-24-25). There they remained until Moses gave them his last message of counsel and encouragement. After completing his farewell sermon, Moses went up "to Mt. Nebo to the top of Pisgah which is opposite Jericho" and there, after seeing the promised land, he died; the Lord buried him, "but no man knows the place of his burial to this day" (Deut. 34:6).

Thus, after a sojourn of hundreds of years in Egypt and a camping trip of over 40 years in the desert, God's people finally returned to the land of Abraham, Isaac, and Jacob (Ex. 12:40). These long hard years had forged a nation that was so closely knit and so strong that no persecution, privation, or calamity of war could destroy them. They still had their weaknesses, but their faith in the one true God, and their loyal obedience to the religious, ceremonial, and civil laws had brought them together as God's chosen people. From out of this fascinating race the promises of God to Abraham, Isaac, and Jacob were to be fulfilled. All of the world would be blessed by the future history of the Hebrew family.

CHAPTER FIVE

The Conquest

Joshua was commissioned to replace Moses as the new leader of his chosen people. During the wanderings in the wilderness, Moses had recognized the leadership ability of Joshua and had asked him to select the men who were to be used against the Amalekites at Rephidim (Ex. 17:8-16). He proved to be such an efficient military leader that the children of Israel won the battle. This was the first step in the rise of Joshua as a leader of Israel. From Ex. 24:13 it appears that Joshua went with Moses to the brow of Sinai during the seven days when the "glory of God" settled on this mountain (Ex. 24:16). It is assumed that he remained behind as Moses made his final ascent to the top of Sinai for his day of encounter with the Lord (Ex. 24:18).

The Amarna Tablets

Joshua was also one of the 12 spies whom Moses sent from the wilderness to see if Canaan could be conquered (Num. 13:1-3, 16, 17). Together with Caleb, Joshua felt

that the Israelites should go in to possess the land. However, the 10 other spies so frightened the people with
their lurid stories of giants that they wouldn't enter the
land (Num. 13:30; 14:6-8). During the 40 ensuing years
of meandering back and forth in the wilderness Joshua's
name is not mentioned. It is assumed, however, that he
must have continued to assist Moses in all of his under-
takings.

It is interesting to note that the name Joshua is referred to in the Amarna Tablets, found in Egypt by a
peasant woman during the winter of 1887-1888. The references to Joshua probably do not refer to the biblical
Joshua, but they do indicate that this Hebrew name
was in common usage at the time.[1] The Amarna Tablets
were letters written by kings of various cities in Canaan
and Syria to Amenhotep III and Amenhotep IV, Egyptian Pharaohs who ruled in about 1400 B.C. In these
letters the Canaanite kings complained about the dis-
order and confusion existing in Canaan. They implied
that many kings were actively engaged in enlarging their
borders at the expense of their neighbors. Each accused
the others of disloyalty and revolt, yet those who wrote
these letters professed their utter devotion to Egypt. The
letters were so filled with accusations against each other
that it appears a political game of intrigue was being
played. Each king was "feathering his own nest" by trying to win the favor of the Egyptians.

Sihon and Og

The first major Israelite battle for control of Palestine
was fought east of the Jordan against Sihon, king of the
Amorites, and Og, king of Bashan. The Israelites asked
for permission to pass through the territory of the Amorites, promising not to "turn aside into field or vineyard;

we will not drink the water of a well; we will go by the King's Highway, until we have passed through your territory" (Num. 21:22). Sihon, king of the Amorites, refused to permit Israel to pass through, so God gave the Amorites into the hands of the Israelites. The victorious Chosen People settled temporarily in their newly conquered territory.

Og, the giant king of Bashan, "came out against" the Israelites next, but the Lord said to Moses, "Do not fear him; for I have given him into your hand, and all his people, and his land" (Num. 21:34). After another victory, the Israelites were free to make plans for the capture of Canaan itself.

The Hittites

The Hittites are mentioned 61 times in the Scriptures. They were a very prominent race of people who became involved in the affairs of the Israelites many times during the days of the Patriarchs and the conquest of Palestine. Egyptian artists depicted these people as having Armenian features. An Egyptian tablet tells of a fierce battle between the Egyptians and the Hittites.

Secular history had left no record of these people, so the existence of such a race had seemed for a time extremely doubtful, and the biblical references to these people were commonly viewed with suspicion. Archeological discoveries, however, have now proved that there was indeed such a nation as the Hittites. The evidence indicates that they were prominent during the time of the Hebrews. The Hittites even took over Egypt for a while, and some of their kings became Pharaohs.[2]

At Boghaz-koi (in modern Turkey), the ancient Hittite capital, an archive of almost 10,000 clay tablets was discovered. This vast store of records has revealed that the Hittites were not only an important people but a

race with an empire that extended to many of the parts
of the known world. It appears that there were two
periods of Hittite domination in Palestine; the first was
about 1900-1800 B.C., while the second period was in 1400-
1200 B.C. One clay tablet tells of a military treaty between
the Hittites and Egyptians nearly 1300 years before the
birth of Jesus.[3]

Abraham purchased the cave of Machpelah as a burial place for his wife from a Hittite (Gen. 23:9-16). Esau
displeased his mother by marrying a daughter of these
foreigners (Gen. 26:34). In the Book of Exodus the Hittites were listed as one of the nations which tried to
resist Joshua. Uriah, the husband of Bathsheba, belonged
to this race. Hittites enlisted in the army of David
(1 Sam. 26:6). Solomon made slaves of these people
and permitted his people to marry their daughters (1
Kings 9:20, 21). God's promise to Joshua was that he
would inherit all the land of the Hittites (Joshua 1:4).
For hundreds of years, the paths of the Hittites and the
Israelites frequently crossed.

Joshua Sends Out Spies

Joshua, like Moses, sent spies into Canaan before he
attempted to lead his people into the promised land.
The Israelites were at that time camped east of the Jordan at Shittim (Joshua 2:1). Josephus, a Jewish historian
who lived at the time of Jesus, refers to a city called
Shittim which lay seven miles east of the river. Pieces of
pottery from the period of 1600-1200 B.C. have been discovered at the site of Shittim, indicating that this city
was occupied during the period of Joshua. The area is
bounded by two streams of water and served as a good
campground for the Israelites. Thus Joshua's spies trav-
eled seven miles westward toward the Jordan and, after

crossing the river, had to go another six miles west to Jericho.

At Jericho the spies were given lodging in the house of Rahab (Joshua 2:1), who hid the men on the roof of her house. Messengers from the king of Jericho were sent to find Joshua's spies, but since Rahab's house was built on the wall of the city, she could lower the two men down from an outside window to freedom. Archeological studies at Jericho indicate that the city was surrounded by a double wall, so that it was possible to construct homes on these ramparts.[4]

Rahab told the spies to flee to the mountains to hide until the soldiers of the king stopped searching for them. Ancient Jericho was located on a plain 14 miles wide; about a mile to the west lay the edge of a rugged plateau which emerged into the central mountain ridge of Palestine. This mountainous area was so high that its shadow covered the city of Jericho in the early hours of the afternoon. The cliff actually rose about 1500 feet above the plain and afforded a good hiding place for the spies. Here Joshua's spies concealed themselves for three days, after which they returned to the Israelite camp across the river to give their report to Joshua.

The Israelites Cross the Jordan

Joshua, hearing the account of the spies, led the Israelites from their camp at Shittim on a seven-mile march to the Jordan. At the crossing point, near the cities of Adam and Zaretan (Jos. 3:16), the Jordan was less than 100 feet wide. When the people arrived, the waters of the Jordan were stopped, permitting them to cross the river bed on dry ground. Since Jericho was about four miles north and west of the Dead Sea, this would give a stretch of at least 20 miles of dry river bed over which Joshua could lead his people into Jericho.

The Scriptures have many picturesque ways of describing this historic crossing of the Jordan. In the Book of Judges we read, "When thou didst march from the region of Edom, the earth trembled" (Judges 5:4). The Psalmist said, "The sea looked and fled, Jordan turned back. The mountains skipped like rams, the hills like lambs" (Ps. 114:3-4). "When those who bore the ark had come to the Jordan, and the feet of the priests bearing the ark were dipped in the brink of the water . . . the waters coming down from above stood and rose up in a heap . . . and those flowing down toward the sea . . . were wholly cut off; and the people passed over opposite Jericho" (Joshua 3:15-16).

Regardless of what happened, the waters of the Jordan ceased flowing so that the chosen people could cross into the Holy Land on dry ground. Joshua and his people, accompanied by the ark of the covenant, now entered a land "flowing with milk and honey." What a wonderful sight the Holy Land must have been for people who had seen nothing but sand, barren mountains, and desert areas for so long a time. Palestine has never been overly fruitful, yet it seemed a paradise for the wanderers who crossed the Jordan to make a new home for themselves. The release from the bondage of Egypt and the gift of a good land in which to live was considered by the Israelites as one of God's greatest blessings.

The Conquest of Canaan

The Hebrews entered Canaan when the world had no strong empires; even Egypt was at a low ebb at the time of the Exodus. This absence of aggressive world kingdoms was very important for the conquest of Canaan by the Israelites and for their rise to nationhood, for it gave Israel a chance to come into being and to establish its own way of life unimpeded by suspicious enemies. Such city-states of Palestine as Jericho, Bethel, Ai, Lachish, Hebron, Eglon, Jarmuth, and Jerusalem were not strong. Even the Philistines were dormant and unaggressive. Israel, then, had a tremendous opportunity to conquer the land and establish her kingdom.

Joshua's conquest of Palestine called for three major phases of attack. First, he had to secure a foothold in central Palestine by conquering Jericho and Ai. The second part of the plan was to subdue the southern part of the Holy Land, and the third phase was to move north to take over Galilee and the northern sections of the land. The fulfillment of these three aims involved a long process of battles, political maneuverings, and conquests led by Joshua, followed by the struggles of the individual tribes as they conquered their respective territories. Joshua destroyed the system of the city-states in Palestine so that the tribes might be free to acquire certain portions of the land and to subjugate most of their enemies.

Jericho

Squarely in the path of the conquest of the Holy Land lay the fortified city of Jericho. No one could conquer central Palestine without first defeating this ancient fortress, which would face the Israelites as soon as they crossed the River Jordan. God directed Joshua to organize the Hebrews in a military formation to march around the city of Jericho once a day for six days and on the seventh day to march around the fortress seven times; then, to the blasting of trumpets and loud shouting of the people, "the walls came tumbling down" (Joshua 6:3-20).

Jericho was one of the most fascinating cities of Palestine. Lying as it did squarely before the eastern entrance to Palestine and the capital city of Jerusalem, it was subject to siege from the Bedouin tribes and the desert nations living east of the Jordan River. Ever since time began this city lay as the direct eastern gateway to the Holy Land. All enemies from the east realized that gaining Palestine would have to involve the destruction of Jericho.

In fact, there are indications that at least five different cities had been built on this particular site, an oasis by the Jordan River. The Jericho of the Neolithic period was constructed during the time from the Stone Age up to 4500 B.C. A later Chalcolithic period Jericho occupied this site from 4500 to 3000 B.C. An Early Bronze Age Jericho thrived from 3000 to 2000 B.C. The Middle Bronze Age Jericho rose and fell during 2000-1500 B.C. Joshua's Jericho was built sometime in the Late Bronze Age, from 1500 to 1200 B.C. Any later city built on this site has been obliterated completely by erosion and the elements.[5]

In 1952 the British School of Archeology and the American School of Oriental Research began an intensive study of the site of Jericho under the direction of Dr. Kathleen Kenyon. Dr. Kenyon discovered that all that remained of the city Joshua conquered was the foundation of a single wall with about a square metre of intact floor beside it; on the floor was a small clay oven with a juglet lying beside it.[6]

This evidence indicates that a city did exist here in Joshua's time. Erosion had taken its toll of the fallen city and erased nearly all of the other artifacts of the Jericho Joshua destroyed. The mound suffered extensive denudation from winter winds, rain, and other forces of nature. The discovery of the little oven still in place indicates that the city had been abandoned; otherwise the oven would have been leveled in the rebuilding of a new city.

According to the Scriptures, Joshua placed a curse upon the city, saying, "Cursed before the Lord be the man that rises up and rebuilds this city, Jericho.

At the cost of his first born shall he lay
its foundations,
And at the cost of his youngest son shall
he set up its gates" (Joshua 6:26).
It is possible that the city of Jericho was abandoned for some four hundred years before it was ever rebuilt.[7] The present city of Jericho lies to the east and south of the site of Joshua's Jericho.

Ai

Having conquered Jericho, Joshua sent 3000 Israelites to capture a stronghold called Ai, 15 miles northwest of Jericho. In their first attempt, these Israelites were defeated. The Bible traces the failure to a disobedient Hebrew named Achan who had disobeyed God's command and stole some gold and silver from Jericho (Joshua 7:1-21). The folly of Achan could not be ignored, and retribution came swiftly. After Achan had been punished by stoning for his sin, Joshua was told by God that his army would then be victorious.

Joshua led the warriors of Ai into a trap by placing a large ambush between Bethel and Ai (Joshua 8:3-12). He then took his main army north of Ai so that the natives could see them and come out to attack the invaders. The Israelites pretended to flee so the soldiers of Ai would come out against them. The fleeing Israelites headed toward the valley of the Jordan River, pursued by the soldiers of Ai. The Israelites who were hidden in ambush between Bethel and Ai came out of their hiding and set fire to the deserted city. Joshua, seeing the city set on fire, turned his forces about and caught an unsuspecting army of Ai in a pincers movement between the main Israelite army and the soldiers who had come out of ambush. Another city had fallen.

The Hivites

After the defeat of the people of Ai, a group of Canaanites known as Hivites came to Joshua to press for peace. They realized that they could never defend themselves against the Hebrew invaders, so they concocted a disguise by wearing old shoes, old clothing, and carrying dry and moldy bread for their provisions (Joshua 9:3-15). Joshua, feeling sorry for these worn-looking travelers, made peace with them and promised not to attack their cities. Later he discovered their deception and learned that these ragged travelers had really come from the four cities of Gibeon, Chephirah, Beeroth, and Kiriath-jearim, just a few miles northwest of Jerusalem. Even though the treaty was obtained by deception, the Israelites felt obligated to respect it, and they did so.

The Southern Coalition

Another group of Canaanite cities, Jerusalem, Hebron, Eglon, Lachish, and Jarmuth, heard of the peace Joshua had made with the Gibeonites. They were angered by this action of the four Gibeonite cities, so, forming a coalition, they declared war on them. The Gibeonites, relying on their peace treaty with Joshua, pleaded for him to come to their rescue. Joshua made a night march against the southern coalition (Joshua 10:5-23).

It was during this battle that the miracle of the "sun standing still" took place, which enabled the Israelites to gain the upper hand (Joshua 10:12-14). The five kings, their armies in a disorganized array of defeat, hid themselves in a cave at Makkedah, where they were caught by Joshua and killed (Joshua 10:16-27). Having conquered these five cities also, Joshua was in control of the greater part of the southern section of Palestine. Now he was ready for the third part of his plan to conquer Canaan, namely the conquest of northern Palestine.

The Northern Coalition

The northern Canaanites also formed a defensive coalition in the face of the advancing Hebrews. The leader of the group was Jabin, then king of the city of Hazor, about 10 miles northwest of the Sea of Galilee (Joshua 11:1). Archeological studies have since shown that Hazor was one of the largest cities of that era, with a population of about 40,000 people. Under God's direction, the Israelites defeated this northern coalition by burning Hazor to the ground. John Garstang, who studied the site carefully, believes that he has found evidence indicating that Hazor was burned between 1400 and 1300 B.C. The kind of evidence found at Hazor is not unique; several of the cities taken in the conquest of the Holy Land have been excavated. Studies of the sites of Jericho, Lachish, Bethel, and Hazor all indicate that they were violently destroyed about the time of Joshua's conquest of Canaan.[8]

The Amarna Tablets have also helped illuminate the conquest of Palestine by Joshua. Seven of these tablets were written by the king of Jerusalem, while others were inscribed by the kings of Tyre and Sidon; several of them tell of the invasion of a group of people called the "Habiru." Many biblical scholars believe the "Habiru" were actually the Hebrews under Joshua.[9]

Dividing the Land

Having completed the conquest of Palestine, Joshua proceeded to parcel out the land of the 12 tribes. The tribe of Levi received no specified area of Palestine; they were the religious leaders, so they divided themselves among the other tribes. To maintain the number 12, Joseph's portion was given to the descendants of his two sons, Ephraim and Manasseh. Thus the 12 new states of Palestine were named after the 10 sons of Jacob and the two sons of Joseph. Two tribes were given land "beyond the Jordan," namely Reuben and Gad. Manasseh was given land on both sides of the river. Thus it is often said that two and one-half tribes of Israel lived beyond the river and nine and one-half tribes lived west of the Jordan.

Joshua fought against 31 kings in his conquest of Canaan. In so small a land, this seems astounding; however, it must be remembered that they were all kings of city-states. As it was, Joshua's conquest of Palestine was still not complete! There were many pockets of resistance which were still unconquered. "There remains yet very much land to be possessed" (Joshua 13:1-7). Joshua, however, did achieve a peace which lasted long enough for the Israelites to settle down and make a home for themselves in the promised land. How wonderful it must have been for the Hebrew pilgrims finally to have a home and land of their own. God's promises to Abraham, Isaac, and Jacob had finally been fulfilled. The seeds of a faith in the one true God were sown. Social, religious, and civil laws were laid down which bound the Israelites into a closely knit nation. God was at work fulfilling his promises.

CHAPTER SIX

The Period of the Judges

The Book of Judges tells the story of the Hebrew people as they established themselves in their new homeland following the initial conquest of Palestine. During the 12th and most of the 11th centuries B.C., the Israelites were busy consolidating their position in Palestine and struggling against the Canaanites who were suspicious of the Hebrews' firm position in the land. The Israelites were beginning to become a settled people; they were living in their designated areas, taking up agriculture, and establishing their homes.

There was a striking difference between the political organization of the Israelites and that of their neighbors. Most of the Canaanites belonged to independent city-states, each with its own petty king. The Israelites had no unifying tie except a loose confederacy held together only by a religious "covenant." The Israelites were in constant danger of attack from their neighbors.

Israel in a State of Flux

Archeologists are agreed that the period of the judges was one of the most hectic and disturbing periods in the history of the Israelites. Excavations of many of the cities of Palestine indicate that they were built, destroyed, and rebuilt two or three times during the years from 1360 B.C. to 1000 B.C. Bethel was sacked at least four times in these centuries. Other cities fared the same fate.

The reason for this unrest was the political upheaval in Palestine while the 12 tribes were trying to consolidate their holdings. There was often conflict between the tribes themselves as they attempted to settle disputed boundaries and land grants. Hostile neighbors who were suspicious of the Israelites added a great deal more confusion.

To the northwest of the Israelites were the Phoenicians; on the coastal plains lived the Philistines; and to the south and southwest were their relatives, the Moabites and the Edomites. It was a marvel that the Israelites survived at all; several times the very existence of this new confederacy hung in the balance.

The Judges

At the beginning of the period of the judges, Joshua was dead, and no leader had been selected to take his place. To defend themselves, the Israelites depended upon the leadership of their own people who were inspired by God to lead them. Without a foe to face, the leadership of Israel was dormant. But when an enemy appeared, God raised up some leader to bring his people to victory.

Israel was ruled for about 350 years by leaders called judges, prophets, or high priests. This age became known as the period of the judges, beginning about 1360 B.C. and continuing until the beginning of the reign of King Saul in 1025 B.C. The history of this period has been recorded in the Book of Judges and the first chapters of 1 Samuel.

These judges were actually military leaders possessed of a divine grace given to them by God; their roles were not at all like those of modern judges. They had wisdom, honesty, insight, and military power which set them apart from ordinary leaders. These judges primarily defended the Israelites from their neighbors in times of war, but they also settled quarrels among the twelve tribes of the weak confederacy. It was in this way that they probably acquired the title of "judge."

Religious Decline of the Hebrews

The Book of Judges is often referred to as the "Book of Failure," and such it is. One of the great tragedies of this 350-year span in the history of the Israelites was the failures the writers of this book saw in the ethical and religious life of the Israelites as they began to settle down in the promised land.

There are several reasons given in Judges and 1 Samuel for this religious failure. In the first place, the Israelites refused to heed God's admonition to drive out the pagans from Palestine. God had given specific instructions that all the unbelievers should be rooted out of Canaan or slain. Some of the idol worshipers, however, were permitted to remain, and they soon corrupted this simple faith the people had known in the wilderness (Judges 1:21-33).

This led to the second reason for Israel's religious decline. The Israelites fell prey to the idolatry of the pagan people they had allowed to remain in Canaan. The law given on Mt. Sinai said, "You shall have no other gods before me. You shall not make yourself a graven image, or any likeness of anything that is in heaven above, or that is in the earth beneath, or that is in the water under the earth" (Ex. 20:4-5). During the period of the Judges, this law was forgotten, and many Israelites adopted the religions of their pagan Canaanite neighbors (Judges 2:12-13).

The third reason for the spiritual decline of God's chosen people was their intermarriage with the native Canaanites (Judges 3:5-6). Pagan wives brought idolatry right into Israelite homes. In addition, the political disunity of the 12 tribes and the frequent intertribal warfare often undermined the strength of the tribes' common religious bonds.

The Rise and Fall of God's People

God raised at least 15 leaders for his people during these troubled 3½ centuries. These leaders of the Israelites were:

1.	Othniel	(Judges 3:7-11)
2.	Ehud	(Judges 3:12-20)
3.	Shamgar	(Judges 3:31)
4.	Deborah	(Judges 4:1—5:31)
5.	Barak	(Judges 4:1—5:31)
6.	Gideon	(Judges 6:1—8:35)
7.	Tola	(Judges 10:1-2)
8.	Jair	(Judges 10:3-5)
9.	Jephthah	(Judges 11:1—12:7)
10.	Ibzen	(Judges 12:8-10)
11.	Elon	(Judges 12:11-12)
12.	Abdon	(Judges 12:13-15)
13.	Samson	(Judges 13:1—16:37)
14.	Eli, the High Priest	(1 Sam. 1:9—4:18)
15.	Samuel, the Prophet	(1 Sam. 3:1—15:4)

The characteristic phrase found in the Book of Judges is "And the people of Israel did what was evil in the sight of the Lord." The book is written almost as if from a formula: each time the people did evil and turned from the Lord, God raised up one of their pagan neighbors to punish the Israelites and to bring them to repentance. When the people repented and turned again to the Lord, he sent a leader from their own group, who served as a judge, military leader, or prophet to deliver his people from their oppressor.

This sequence of apostasy, servitude, and deliverance occurs seven times in the Book of Judges!

1. The "People of Israel did what was evil in the sight of the Lord, forgetting the Lord their God." Mesopotamia was sent by God to oppress the people for eight years during the first apostasy. Othniel was the Judge whom God raised up as a military leader to free his people from the King of Mesopotamia. The "Spirit of the Lord" descended on Othniel so that he was able to overcome the enemy and to establish a peace for 40 years (Judges 3:7-11).

2. "And the people of Israel again did what was evil in the sight of the Lord." The King of Moab was permitted to invade western Palestine in order to oppress the Israelites for 18 years. This brought Israel to repentance, so God "raised up" Ehud as a leader to free the Israelites from the oppression of the Moabite King. Ehud assassinated King Eglon of Moab and gave the Israelites peace for 80 years (Judges 3:12-30).

3. "And the people of Israel again did what was evil in the sight of the Lord." The third oppression came at the hand of Jabin, King of the Canaanites, the most formidable of all of the enemies of Israel; his capital was Hazor. King Jabin's 900 chariots of iron terrorized the Israelites. When they repented, God used Deborah, a prophetess and judge of her people, and Barak, her military general, to free his people from the oppression of the Canaanites under King Jabin of Hazor. Deborah's

famous song, in Judges 5:1-31, gives a poetic account of this event.

Deborah's career marks a significant milestone in the transition from Israel's tribal life toward its existence as a united nation. The organized resistance of the Canaanites ceased, though a number of independent Canaanite towns still remained to be captured by the Israelites (Judges 4:1-31).

4. "The people of Israel did what was evil in the sight of the Lord." During this fourth apostasy, God used the Midianites, a camel-riding nomadic people who made periodic raids against the Israelites. During the harvest season they carried off the newly harvested crops and the herds of sheep, goats, and oxen. God sent Gideon to deliver the Israelites from the seven years of oppression by the Midianites. Gideon was offered hereditary rule by the Israelites, but he declined the honor; he felt that God alone was the ruler of his people (Judges 6:1—8:32).

5. "And the people of Israel again did what was evil in the sight of the Lord." Now the Ammonites came; they oppressed the Israelites for 18 years. This time God chose Jephthah, because of his ability and initiative, to be the military leader to free his people from the oppression of the Ammonites (Judges 10:6—12:7).

6. "And the people of Israel again did what was evil in the sight of the Lord." During their seventh apostasy God permitted the Philistines to oppress his people for 40 years. Samson arose as the leader of Israel during this long and difficult oppression (Judges 13:1—16:37). According to the Bible, Samson met his death in the temple of Dagon, where he was able by his regained strength to pull down the two middle pillars of the temple and thereby destroy the whole building filled with pagan worshipers. Excavations have shown that some of

the large Philistine buildings were built around a central hall which was held up by pillars, used to support the roof and the upper story.

Eli

Eli, the priest, served as a political leader in addition to his religious responsibilities. When the people had differences, they came to him to settle their problems. But Eli was not even able to train and control his own sons, and did not prove to be a very wise or capable leader. Because of Eli's failure, the priestly office was taken from him, and he and his sons died at the same time, fulfilling God's warning (1 Sam. 3:10-15).

Samuel

Samuel is probably best remembered as a prophet; however, he also served as a judge (1 Sam. 7:6). In fact, Samuel was actually considered the last of the Judges. Eli, the priest who trained Samuel for his office as prophet and judge, fell backwards and died when he received the message that the Hebrew Ark of the Covenant had been taken by their enemy, the Philistines, and that his two wayward sons were slain in battle (1 Sam. 4:12-13). This left Samuel as both political and spiritual leader of all 12 of the Hebrew tribes.

The Ark of God

In the Bible account the Philistines did not fare very well with the Ark of God. When they placed it in their temple, the Philistine idol, Dagon, fell flat on its face before the Ark. The Philistines raised the statue up again, only to discover the next morning that their idol had fallen once more, and this time the hands had broken off (1 Samuel 5:1-7). After a series of misfortunes, the Philistines were happy to get rid of the Ark and return it to the rightful owners, the Israelites.

Temples dedicated to the worship of the god Dagon had been discovered in archeological studies of Palestine. It appears that Dagon was worshiped as a deity as early as 2500 B.C. The Ras Shamra Tablets give evidence that Dagon was the grain god of the Philistines. A modern Arab village is still called Beit Dajan, or "House of Dagon," after the Philistine deity.[1]

Archeological discoveries have confirmed the accuracy of the apostasy, oppression, and deliverance of God's people during these years of failure. Some of the names of the leaders of these oppressions have been discovered in the Ras Shamra Tablets; the best evidence indicates that they fit into the period of the Judges. The Amarna Tablets confirm the fact that the Israelites did not drive out all the Canaanites from the land as God had asked them to do; the Jebusites living in Jerusalem, for example, remained in their mountain-top fortress throughout this period. Archeological excavations reveal that the city of Bethel, 10 miles north of Jerusalem, was destroyed by fire three times during the period of the Judges.[2] Studies at the site of Hazor indicate that the city was in existence during the days of the Judges, and that it too was destroyed during this time.[3]

When Abimelech wanted to avenge himself on the men of Shechem, he attacked the city and burned the fortress in order to destroy everyone in the city. Archeological studies of pottery discovered in these burned ruins indicate that the fortress had been built about 1300 B.C. and was destroyed by fire in 1150 B.C.[4]

The power of the Philistines can be determined from

a study of the monuments of Ramses III of Egypt. The Philistines attempted to land in the rich delta area of Egypt. When attacked and defeated by Ramses III, the Philistines went back to Palestine.[5]

No Smith in Israel

It is quite natural to expect that the period of the Judges, when Israel was weak and disunited, should not yield an exciting amount of archeological remains. Nevertheless, the artifacts which have been found from this period do confirm the weaknesses of the 12 tribes during these years. Everywhere the domination of the Philistines and the impotence of the Israelites are evident.

Before 1200 B.C. iron was a rare commodity, almost as valuable as silver and gold. The earliest people to work with iron were the Hittites and the Philistines, who jealously guarded their secret process of smelting iron ore. The Scriptures verify this, "Now there was no smith to be found throughout all the land of Israel; for the Philistines said, 'Lest the Hebrews make themselves swords or spears'; but every one of the Israelites went down to the Philistines to sharpen his plowshare, his mattock, his axe, or his sickle" (1 Sam. 13:19-20).

Iron weapons gave the enemies of Israel a great advantage over their neighbors, for excavations indicate that the Hittites and the Philistines possessed iron weapons and tools before the Israelites acquired them. The Book of Joshua tells of how the Israelites feared the chariots of iron (Joshua 17:16). Sisera, the commander of the army of the Canaanite king, Jabin, had 900 chariots of iron (Judges 4:3). The archeological remains of Israelite homes indicate how devoid these people were of art forms and smelted iron. Their houses were simple, crude, and small. Only King Saul and his son Jonathan had swords in the Hebrew army (Judges 5:8, 1 Sam. 13:22).

Archeology does reveal that the Israelites learned the art of building cisterns, and plastered them with lime in order to make them waterproof. This made it possible for the Hebrews to live in places where there were no rivers, streams, or natural bodies of water.

In spite of all the disruptive forces at work during the period of the Judges to disturb the Israelites' consolidation, there were a few redeeming features. The Israelites had a common language, a common religion, and a common law which held them together. They had a sanctuary at Shiloh which helped to keep them in one fold. Their many traditions and customs were unifying influences. God always raised a leader when it was necessary; he blessed and prospered the people when they were faithful to his demands. Most importantly, Samuel, the last of the great judges of Israel, gave in to the requests of his people for a king. He anointed Saul, who became the first monarch of Israel. Through this act God's people truly became a nation, with a king like their Canaanite and Philistine neighbors. Even if God opposed this new venture, the Israelites had high hopes that their new king would lead them into a victorious and glorious future.

CHAPTER SEVEN

The United Kingdom

Israel made several attempts at choosing a king that would be acceptable to all twelve tribes. The most familiar of the experiments in kingship was the attempt of the tribes to make Gideon their king. Gideon was successful in driving out of Palestine the Midianites, a camel-riding, marauding nomadic enemy, which harassed the land by carrying off crops, sheep, goats, and whatever they could seize. Gideon handled the situation so well they offered to make him king. However, Gideon's reply was, "I will not rule over you, and my son will not rule over you; the Lord will rule over you" (Judges 8:23). A second attempt at kingship was that of Gideon's son Abimelech, who conspired with the men of Shechem, and after killing his seventy brothers, ruled for three years. However, a woman dropped a millstone on his head and thus ended the second attempt of the Israelites to form a monarchy (Judges 9:6–10:57).

During the days of Samuel the Hebrews begged for a king. Samuel knew this was not God's will, yet, after much persistence on the part of the Israelites, God revealed to the prophet that he should give in to their demand. Samuel unwillingly anointed Saul, first in a private ceremony (1 Sam. 10:1) and later in a public service at Mizpah (1 Sam. 10:14-25), as the first king of the Hebrews.

Saul

Saul established the city of Gibeah, located three miles north of Jerusalem, as his capital. Excavations at Gibeah indicate that Saul built an interesting palace as his residence. This palace was strongly fortified and appeared more like a fortress than a royal palace. However, since Saul was primarily a warrior who "from his shoulders upward . . . was taller than any of the people" it would be natural that his residence would have a militaristic appearance (1 Sam. 9:2). The palace Saul built was a two-story structure with the family living quarters on the second floor. In the ruins of the palace were discovered bronze arrows, sling stones, grind stones, whetstones, blackened cooking utensils, storage jars, and an iron plowpoint.[1] Thus the home of Saul was undoubtedly simple, in keeping with the tastes of a warrior king. A thick double wall surrounded the palace. The outer wall was about six or seven feet thick and constructed of stone. The corners were protected by strong towers. The size of this fortress is not certain, but it was at least 169 feet long and 114 feet wide. It was crude in design but very well built.[2]

Early in his reign Saul disobeyed God by personally offering a sacrifice at Gilgal instead of waiting for Samuel, the prophet, to perform this sacred rite. This was contrary to God's expressed command. Because of this breach of obedience, Saul was told that his kingdom would come to an end and the rule of Israel would not continue in his family (1 Sam. 13:8-15). Saul, in severe depressive states, would call upon David to play the harp and sing for him. David became the court musician.

The music of David quieted King Saul for a while, but his fits of despondency came back time after time. David's life was constantly in danger, as the erratic Saul might throw his javelin at the singing shepherd boy any time. King Saul was very jealous of David's victory over Goliath and spent a great deal of his time trying to slay the young singer. During all these years of struggle between Saul and David, the boy singer returned only love to his anointed king.

Saul's reign was one long struggle against the hostile neighbors that surrounded Israel. His first victory (at Michmash, where he drove back the Philistines) won the utter respect of his people (1 Sam. 14:1-52). Saul also fought against the Ammonites and other enemies of Israel, but when his sons were killed the wounded king took his own life to avoid being captured by his enemies (1 Sam. 31:1-13).

Saul's body was beheaded, he was stripped of his armor, and "word was sent throughout the land of the Philistines, to carry the good news to the people and to their pagan idols" (1 Sam. 31:9). Saul's armor was hung in the temple of the goddess Ashtaroth at Bethshan, and his body was nailed to the city walls (1 Chron. 10:1-14).

Excavations of Bethshan made in 1931-33 have uncovered one of the most complete sites ever found. The piles of debris were 79 feet high, with at least 18 different layers of civilizations. Ruins of the temple of Dagon and Ashtaroth were uncovered. These ancient centers of worship contained numerous articles used in their idol worship.[3] It was in one of these two temples where the head of Saul was placed. The city appeared to have been burned about the time of David.

King Saul's reign lasted only about 15 years. He imposed no taxes upon his people; his main achievement as king was to harass and hold down the enemies of Israel.

David

David rose to fame by slaying the Philistine giant Goliath. The sling David used was not the forked stick of modern times; David's sling was a little leather pouch with two long cords attached to either end. A smooth round stone was placed in the pouch. Holding the cords in the hand, a man would deftly whirl the sling around his head at a terrific speed until he released one of the strings and sent the pebble flying into the air. David's family tribe, Judah, had a platoon of "700 picked men who were left-handed; every one could sling a stone at a hair and not miss" (Judges 20:16). The stones used in these slings were about two or three inches in diameter and made of hard flint or lime. The sling was one of the chief weapons of war in this agrarian period of history.

David, the singing shepherd boy, was anointed by men of Judah who came up to Hebron to make David their next king (2 Sam. 2:3-5). David's ascent to the throne of Israel ushered in the most spectacular age that Israel ever experienced; it has been designated by most historians as the "Golden Age" of Israel. It was during the reigns of David and his successor Solomon that Israel became a nation of great significance.

David, however, had competition in his ascent to the throne. One of Saul's military leaders placed Ishbosheth, the fourth son of King Saul, on the throne to be the next king (2 Sam. 2:8). For a while Israel had two kings, but this arrangement lasted only two years, until Ishbosheth was assassinated by his own captains. At the death of Ishbosheth, all of the 12 tribes acknowledged David as their rightful and only king (2 Sam. 5:1-5).

At first David established his capital at Hebron, where he had been anointed. Here he ruled for seven and one-half years (2 Sam. 5:5). The Israelites had never been able to take Jerusalem in their conquests, even though for centuries it had been an important city. King David knew that if he continued to make his capital at Hebron, he would be accused by his people of favoring the southern tribe of Judah. If he chose a city to the north, the same accusation would be made by the southern tribes. David realized that it would be very important for his permanent capital to be located in a neutral area, more toward the center of his domain; Jerusalem appeared to be an ideal choice. He planned to capture the city with his own personal troops so that Jerusalem would belong to him, and him alone; thus his capital would be impartial to both the north and the south.

Jerusalem is surrounded on three sides by steep cliffs, which made it a formidable fortress. When David finally captured the city (the residents had boasted that it could be defended by the lame and the blind), he made Jerusalem his religious and political capital. He constructed his palace in the city and also brought the Ark of the Covenant into Jerusalem (2 Sam. 5).

The Egyptian Pharaohs were too weak to be concerned about David's new kingdom which had arisen so rapidly. Babylon and Assyria were also dormant during David's days, and the Hittites were undergoing a period of decline. David's only opposition came from the internal disunity of the 12 tribes. The lack of external pressure left David free to unite his domain and to establish Jerusalem firmly as his capital.

David soon began to feel uneasy because the Ark of the Covenant was housed in a tent while he himself lived in a house of cedar. It was one of David's greatest ambitions to build a temple for his God. However, the Lord revealed to David through the prophet Nathan that this temple would be built by David's son, since David had been such a warrior. God promised David that his kingdom would last forever, that his throne would always have a successor (2 Sam. 7:7-16).

David defeated the Philistines, the Moabites, the Syrians, the Edomites, and the Ammonites (2 Sam. 8:1-14, 10:7-8). In addition to all his military achievements, however, David encouraged the advances which were made in commerce, trade, and international affairs. David consolidated the 12 tribes, destroyed their enemies, and established the greatest Israelite nation in all history. His government was well organized and highly developed. It is no wonder that his reign is still remembered as the "Golden Age of Israel."

Progress During the Golden Age

Since David was more of a warrior than a builder, archeological discoveries from his age have been few. Nevertheless, what evidence there is does indicate the prosperity that David's reign brought to his people after the defeat of his enemies. The Hebrews learned the art of smelting iron; for the first time, iron plows were available to the Hebrew farmer. Pruning hooks and sickles replaced the crude stone implements which Israelites had used up to this time. Iron nails were used in building homes. David also "built up great stores of iron for nails and clamps, as well as bronze in quantities beyond weighing and cedar timbers without numbers" for the temples which Solomon, his son, would build (1 Chron.

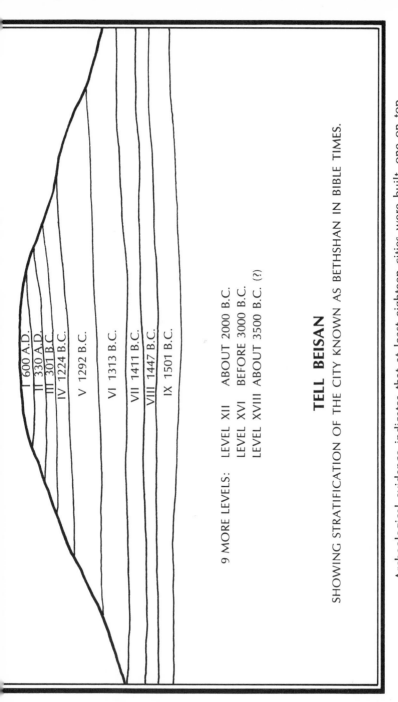

I 600 A.D.
II 330 A.D.
III 301 B.C.
IV 1224 B.C.
V 1292 B.C.
VI 1313 B.C.
VII 1411 B.C.
VIII 1447 B.C.
IX 1501 B.C.

9 MORE LEVELS: LEVEL XII   ABOUT 2000 B.C.
LEVEL XVI   BEFORE 3000 B.C.
LEVEL XVIII ABOUT 3500 B.C. (?)

TELL BEISAN

SHOWING STRATIFICATION OF THE CITY KNOWN AS BETHSHAN IN BIBLE TIMES.

Archeological evidence indicates that at least eighteen cities were built, one on top of the other at the site of ancient Bethshan.

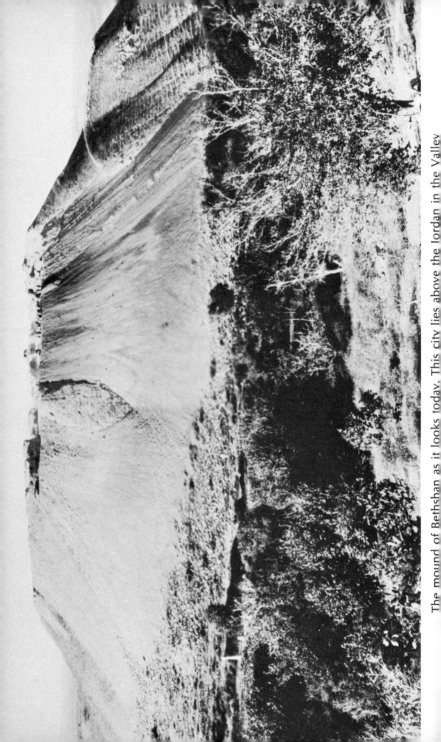

The mound of Bethshan as it looks today. This city lies above the Jordan in the Valley

A photographer takes a picture of a mortar which was probably used by a Hebrew housewife to grind grain. The tags on the walls indicate different levels or strata.

An exciting moment in an archeological discovery. A brush is used to carefully un-

The great stables of King Solomon at Megiddo. It has been estimated that this stable had room for as many as five hundred horses.

(Photo, courtesy of the Oriental Institute, University of Chicago)

The Moabite Stone commemorating the vic-

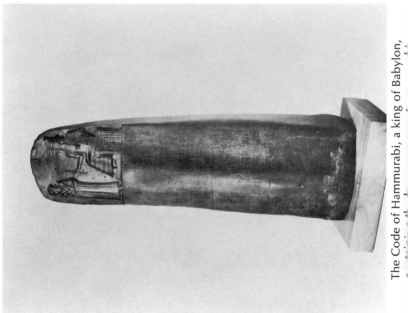

The Code of Hammurabi, a king of Babylon,

The Rosetta Stone discovered in Egypt in 1798. This stone
helped decipher the hieroglyphical writing of ancient Egypt.

(British Museum Photo)

The Black Obelisk of Shalmaneser III com-

One of the jars from Cave One at Qumran

Two pillars from a temple built in the city of Samaria by Herod the Great.

(Photo by Adelbert Bartlett)

The ruins of an ancient Jewish synagogue on the site of Capernaum probably con-

These ruins are all that remain of the once magnificent city of Babylon built by Nebuchadnezzar.

(Religious News Service Photo)

The "Fields of Boaz" in Bethlehem where Ruth gleaned barley. Here David cared for
his flocks, and somewhere in the vicinity the shepherds received their announcement

Scenes from the ancient city of Gibeon, eight miles north-west of Jerusalem: A tunnel cut from solid rock, connected the city with a spring outside the city wall *(top left)*. A pottery jar removed from a tomb near Gibeon *(top right)*. A portion of the massive inner wall of Gibeon *(bottom)*.

(Religious News Service Photo)

The ancient walls of Jericho. "By faith the walls of Jericho fell down after they had

Jebel Musa, Arabic "Mount Moses," in the southern part of the Sinai Peninsula. This is the traditional Mount Sinai.

The Dead Sea at sunrise. This lake is a massive cauldron of saturated salt solution, with a density five times greater than the oceans of the world.

(Three Lions Photo)

22:3). "He set stone cutters to prepare dressed stones for building the house of God" (1 Chron. 22:2).

Archeological evidence also indicates a general increase in population. Permanent homes built of wood and stone were developed, providing the first permanent homes for the Israelites. The pottery used by the Hebrews became far more artistic. A higher standard of living was developed for God's chosen people, giving them for the first time a sense of prosperity. The literature of this age reveals a remarkable genius in writing. On every front the Israelites' culture advanced at a rapid pace.

Perhaps one of the greatest contributions of Israel to the entire world of that time was its music. Archeological monuments have revealed that Palestine was well known throughout the Near East for its music.[4] For many centuries the Holy Land was a land where music was deeply appreciated. Tombs, vases, tablets, and stelae show Semites coming into Egypt with musical instruments. As early as 1900 B.C. Egyptian artists painted Hebrews visiting their land, carrying musical instruments with them. The harp, lyre, oboe, and trumpet were all in common use. The archeological monuments of Egypt, Mesopotamia, and Phoenicia all indicate a high development of musical instruments and their use during the time of David. Hebrew singers were prominent in all the known world of David's day.[5]

Declining Years of David

David reigned for 40 years as King (1010-971), but, tragically enough, the last years of his reign were beclouded by sin, rebellion, spoiled children, tragedy, famine, infirmity, and sorrow. Even the greatest of Israel's kings could not escape the consequences of sin.

On his deathbed David ordered that the priest should anoint his son Solomon as the next king of Israel (1 Kings 1:32-40). Before his death David pleaded with Solomon to walk in the ways of the Lord (1 Kings 2:2-4).

Solomon

The reign of Solomon continued and expanded this most flourishing period in the history of Palestine. It was his privilege to make a great nation from the newly united tribes. The Lord had blessed Solomon in many ways; the United Kingdom of Israel now extended from "the Euphrates to the land of the Philistines and to the border of Egypt" (1 Kings 4:21).

Solomon began the construction of the temple at Jerusalem. King Hiram of Tyre furnished the "hewn" stones and cedar for the building (1 Kings 5:10). Archeological data has made it possible to reconstruct the building to a fair degree of accuracy—the temple was probably about 90 feet long, 30 feet wide, and 30 feet high. It was divided into two large rooms—the Most Holy Place was a cube about 30 feet on a side, while the Holy Place was approximately 50 feet long, 30 feet high, and 30 feet wide. The temple was probably built entirely of stone, but it was lined on the inside with highly decorated and carved cedar. This cedar lining was, in turn, overlaid with pure gold (1 Kings 6:16-22).

A large porch, 30 feet long and 15 feet wide, was built across the front of this great temple. At the sides of the door of the edifice stood two huge, highly decorated and carved pillars of bronze (1 Kings 7:15-22). In front of the porch and the two pillars of the temple stood the great bronze sea, which was a tremendous bowl 15 feet in diameter and 7½ feet high; this had been cast entirely of bronze to a thickness of three inches. This great bowl rested on the backs of 12 oxen which were arranged in groups of three, facing the four corners of the world. Computations indicate that this great sea weighed from 25 to 30 tons; it held 10,000 gallons of water for sacramental washings and ablutions (1 Kings 7:23-37).[6]

This beautiful temple, built by King Solomon, was completely destroyed by the Babylonians under King Nebuchadnezzar; no trace of it has ever been uncovered.

Remains of many of Solomon's buildings have been found at Megiddo, Gezer, and Eglon. The excavations at Megiddo have probably been the most extensive ever carried out in Palestine; the work was begun in 1925 and continued for 10 years by the University of Chicago. The archeological excavations at Megiddo indicate that even the stables of Solomon were well built, having been constructed of stone and lined with cedar. The stables were arranged in double rows and equipped with stone pillars which served as posts for tying the horses. Stone mangers were built to feed the horses; the floors were paved with rough stones to prevent the horses from slipping. The stables at Megiddo were large enough to house at least 450 horses.

In 1938-1940 an archeologist, Nelson Glueck, discovered Ezion-geber, a flourishing city in Solomon's day. The site is located on the plains of the Jordan near the Persian Gulf, where Solomon had his furnaces for smelting copper and iron (1 Kings 7:46). The smelter here is the largest ever to be discovered in the Near East.

Ezion-geber lies in the path of the constantly prevailing north winds which created a forced draft for the smelting furnaces.[7] Nelson Glueck has called Ezion-geber the "Pittsburgh of Palestine" making Solomon "a copper king."[8]

Near this refinery were great walled camps to house the slave workers in the smelter. The Scriptures even speak of Solomon's fleet of ships which brought gold, silver, ivory, apes, and peacocks to his realm (1 Kings 10:22). Ezion-geber became Solomon's major seaport, and here he sent out his ships to bring back the riches of the East. The Bible tells us that Solomon had a "navy of Tarshish" located here (1 Kings 10:22). A "Tarshish fleet" may have been a refinery fleet, since the origin of the word "Tarshish" is very vague.

The Queen of Sheba in southern Arabia heard of Solomon's glory and wealth. Eager to behold the splendor of Solomon's kingdom, she came to Palestine with a great camel caravan, bearing gifts of precious stones, spices, and gold (1 Kings 10:1-2). The Queen discovered that the wisdom and prosperity of Solomon exceeded all of her expectations. "I did not believe the reports until I came and my own eyes had seen it; and, behold, the half was not told me; your wisdom and prosperity surpass the report which I heard" (1 Kings 10:7).

Solomon's Decline

Early in his reign King Solomon cemented a political alliance with Egypt by marrying a daughter of Pharaoh (1 Kings 3:1). Later Solomon married other foreign wives, many of whom turned his heart from worship of the true God. He even constructed temples for pagan deities to please his heathen wives (1 Kings 11:7-8). Archeologists have discovered a seal impression of the goddess Ashtoreth at Bethel where Jacob had built his altar to the Lord, indicating that pagan worship was established by King Solomon even on this historic sacred site.

King Solomon impoverished his nation by building so many mighty cities, fleets, and mines. He was forced to turn over 20 Galilean cities to King Hiram of Tyre to pay his debts incurred in building his temples and houses. Solomon taxed his people harshly, creating discontent and the seeds of rebellion. By the end of his reign, Israel's king had nearly destroyed his success, and left little but discontent for his successors.

CHAPTER EIGHT

The Divided Kingdom

After the death of Solomon in 931 B.C., his son Rehoboam took over the reign of the kingdom. The Israelites had suffered from the heavy taxation during the extensive building program of Solomon, and they pleaded with Rehoboam to make their burden easier. Rehoboam foolishly listened to the counsel of his young advisors, and told his people, "Whereas my father laid upon you a heavy yoke, I will add to your yoke. My father chastised you with whips, but I will chastise you with scorpions" (1 Kings 12:11). This attitude on the part of the new king angered the 10 northern tribes of Israel and caused them to secede from the union, choosing Jeroboam as their new king. This new nation became known as the kingdom of Israel (the Northern Kingdom), with Shechem as its capital. It lasted only about 200 years and was ruled during that time by 19 kings. Only two tribes remained faithful to Solomon's son, King Rehoboam; they became known as the kingdom of Judah, or the Southern Kingdom, retaining the descendants of David as their rulers. The boundary between the two nations was the northern border of the old tribe of Benjamin, 10 miles north of Jerusalem.

Jeroboam

Jeroboam, the new king of the 10 northern tribes, realized that it would be unwise for his people to continue worshiping at the temple in Jerusalem, since it was also the political capital of the Southern Kingdom. The Jerusalem temple could encourage his people to remain loyal to Rehoboam, so that Jeroboam would lose his throne. To prevent this possibility, Jeroboam made two golden calves and set them up in two worship centers in his own territory. One was at Dan, located north of the Sea of Galilee, and the other one at Bethel, just 10 miles north of Jerusalem.

In these two worship centers, according to the biblical account, calf worship was established. Jeroboam said to his people, "You have gone to Jerusalem long enough. Behold your gods, O Israel, who brought you up out of the land of Egypt" (1 Kings 12:28). He appointed priests who were not of the tribe of Levi to offer sacrifices at these worship centers.

Worship of animals was common in Egypt at this time. A tomb at Memphis, Egypt, was erected in honor of the sacred cow. Jeroboam, who had just returned from a self-imposed exile into Egypt, had perhaps become acquainted with the calf cult practiced there (1 Kings 11:40; 12:2). Now as the newly crowned King of Israel, he introduced this form of worship to his people, connecting it with the Israelites' 430-year sojourn in Egypt.

Some archeological studies have indicated that Jeroboam himself intended the statues merely to define the presence of the God of Israel in the holy palace, but the people easily lapsed into worshiping the statues for their own sake.

Thus Jeroboam succeeded in his plan to keep his people from going down to Jerusalem for worship in the temple. Now they would be isolated from the Southern Kingdom, thus making his throne even more secure.

Because of this great sin of Jeroboam his whole family was utterly destroyed; their bodies were eaten by dogs and birds (1 Kings 14:7-11). Archeological discoveries indicate that Jeroboam's successors were weak, and that the throne of the Northern Kingdom tottered many times. Some of these kings of Israel ruled for only a matter of days or months.

Omri

Omri, the sixth king of Israel, was the first ruler of any significance after Jeroboam. Omri had been an army officer before he seized the throne (1 Kings 16:15-24). Of all the rulers of the Northern Kingdom, he left the deepest imprint on the history of Israel. Omri moved the capital of Israel from Shechem to the city of Samaria, which he founded (1 Kings 16:24). No other site in the whole Northern Kingdom could have provided a capital city of such strength, beauty, and fertility. It even had advantages over Jerusalem as a political center. It was ideally located in the center of the Kingdom of Israel. and made a capital that was practically impregnable.

Samaria was not an old site; archeology has confirmed the fact that Omri was the first to build a city on the mountain of Samaria. Harvard University has excavated the site of the city and found the remains of the large palace built by Omri. Omri hired architects of amazing ability and insight; the ruins of this city reveal the finest construction ever used in Palestine up to this time.[1]

Ahab

Ahab, the seventh king of Israel, married Jezebel, the evil daughter of the king of Sidon. She brought with her from her home in Phoenicia the worship of Baal. Almost immediately the prophets Elijah and Elisha began to warn the people of the sin and dangers of Baal veneration, which in some aspects was an even greater curse than calf worship.

Archeological discoveries show that the word Baal was found many times in connection with the personal names of the people who lived in the Northern Kingdom. Many seals and inscriptions from this period indicate a connection between Baal worship and the Israelites. In the Southern Kingdom, however, the name of Baal is never associated with the Hebrews who lived here. Baal worship, apparently, was a curse of the Northern Kingdom only.

The Scriptures refer to the ivory palace of Ahab (1 Kings 22:39). Excavations at Samaria indicate that Ahab's palace had walls faced with white marble. Numerous ivory decorations were found in the form of plaques, panels, and ornamentations.[2]

Ahab was the first king of the Northern Kingdom to come into contact with the power and might of Assyria. Ahab hurriedly arranged a marriage of his son Ahaziah to a daughter of the king of Judah so that the two nations might unite against Assyria. The Assyrians left a record which says that Ahab of Israel had 2000 chariots and 10,000 soldiers.

The Moabite Stone

An interesting archeological discovery from this period was made in 1860 by a German clergyman, F. A. Klein, who found in the city of Dibon in Moab a stone with unusually legible inscriptions. This stone, called by archeologists the Moabite stone, was a bluish-black basalt rock, two feet wide, four feet high, and 14½ inches thick. An inscription in Phoenician letters of some 34 lines had been carved into the stone.

The Germans tried to obtain the stone for 40 dollars, but during the negotiations with the Arabs the stone was heated and cold water poured over it, so that it broke into many pieces; the Arabs hoped in this way to secure even more profit by selling fragments separately. Most of the pieces were recovered at great expense and with considerable difficulty.

When assembled, the writings on the stone could finally be deciphered. The French government heard about the Moabite stone and sent an agent to make a "squeeze" of the stone (a facsimile impression of the inscriptions). The French government eventually secured possession of the stone for 1500 dollars, and it is now housed in the Louvre Museum in Paris.

The inscriptions on the Moabite Stone indicate that Omri, king of Israel, and his son oppressed and overran the Moabites. Ahab, Omri's son, collected an annual tribute from the Moabites of 100,000 rams.[3]

Jehu

Elisha, the prophet, had Jehu anointed to be king of Israel in order to end the reign of Ahab and his idolatrous family. Jehu set out to take over the kingdom, putting to death the 70 sons of Ahab and most of Ahab's court. Jehu commanded that Jezebel be thrown out of an upper window and killed. The new king put to death the prophets of Baal, burned the images of this pagan deity, and destroyed the temples of Baal. He wiped out Baal worship, but he did permit the worship of the golden calves at Dan and Bethel (2 Kings 9, 10).

Jehu's reign has been confirmed by the discovery of a monument at Nimrud, south of Nineveh in Assyria, called "The Black Obelisk of Shalmaneser III." This obelisk presents the earliest picture of Israelites discovered up to this time. The monument shows Jehu paying tribute and homage to King Shalmaneser III of Assyria. The Black Obelisk also pictures four Hebrew officials and 13 Hebrew porters bearing gifts to the Assyrian king as a tribute to their conqueror. The inscription on the obelisk reads "Tribute of Jehu, the son of Omri: I received from him silver, gold, a golden bowl, a golden vase with painted bottom, golden tumblers, golden bracelets, tin, a staff for a king." This obelisk is now housed in the British Museum.

Jeroboam II

Jehu's son and grandson were weak, insignificant rulers. His great-grandson, Jeroboam II, was far more powerful; "he restored the border of Israel from the entrance of Hamath as far as the Sea of the Arabah" (2 Kings 14:25). (Hamath lay north of Tyre and Sidon.) Jeroboam also subdued the city of Damascus, thus becoming the ruler of all the land north of Judah. His victories ushered in a golden age for the Northern Kingdom.

Amos the prophet, however, took a dim view of this prosperity. He had been a herdsman and a gatherer of sycamore figs, but his exposure to the city life of Samaria made him convinced that he had to call God's judgment upon the Israelites. He had lived in Judah, 10 miles south of Jerusalem at Tekoa, yet he rebuked Jeroboam, the king of Israel. Amos cried out that all the superficial sacrifices and empty rituals of the Israelites were of no avail if the people remained unconcerned by the need for justice among men and unmoved by the pitiable condition of their brothers. He denounced the privileged few who slept on ivory beds while others went naked, and announced that God would judge such a perversion of true religion.

Amos apparently spoke the truth. Archeological searches have shown that many Israelites lived quite luxuriously; furniture with ivory inlay has been found at Samaria, the capital of Israel.

The prophet Hosea was also active during the time of Jeroboam. He, too, saw through the sham religion of the Israelites. God, he proclaimed, requires "steadfast love and not sacrifice, the knowledge of God rather than burnt offerings" (Hosea 6:6). He saw God's wrath about to be expressed against Israel, but still promised that God's love would never completely leave the nation.

The Fall of the Northern Kingdom

After the rule of Jeroboam II, the Kingdom began to dissolve. Some of the succeeding kings were cut down by assassins after a rule of only a few months. Usurpers occupied the throne, one after the other. Finally, sleeping Assyria rose to power; by sheer force and brutality, its kings began to push down into the very gates of the Northern Kingdom. The kings of Israel were forced to pay tribute to Assyria for many years. Before the Northern Kingdom finally fell, their kings were forced to pay as much as $30,000 in gold and $2,000,000 in silver as a yearly tribute to Assyria.

Finally, Shalmaneser V, king of Assyria, besieged Samaria for three years (2 Kings 17:5-6). Shalmaneser died before the capture was completed; it was Sargon II, a general in Assyria's army, who finally destroyed Samaria in 721 B.C. The principal inhabitants of Israel were carried into a captivity from which they never returned. To this day, no one has ever been able to determine what happened to the 10 tribes which made up the Northern Kingdom.

Sargon II fell in battle and was succeeded by his son Sennacherib, who began to harass the remaining Southern Kingdom.

Hezekiah

The Southern Kingdom, with its temple at Jerusalem, was able to maintain its spiritual life and worship of the God of the patriarchs for over 100 years following the fall of the Northern Kingdom. Pagan forms of worship, however, did gradually creep into their religious experience. Hezekiah, though, was a godly king despite the abominations of his wicked father Ahaz. Hezekiah reopened the doors of the temple, resumed the celebration of the Passover feast, and instituted a spiritual awakening which caused the people of the Southern Kingdom to destroy their idols and places of pagan worship. As the biblical account relates, Hezekiah "held fast to the Lord; he did not depart from following him, but kept the commandments which the Lord commanded Moses. And the Lord was with him; wherever he went forth, he prospered" (2 Kings 18:6-7). As a result of this, when the Assyrian king came to besiege Jerusalem, the Lord delivered the city from the hand of the enemy which had just destroyed the Northern Kingdom (Is. 37:33-38).

The Bible tells of a pool and conduit which Hezekiah constructed to bring water into the city of Jerusalem in case of an attack by Assyria (2 Kings 20:20). A few years ago the author walked through the tunnel that still connects the spring of Gihon, which was the chief source of water for ancient Jerusalem, with the pool that Heze-

kiah made at the south end of the city. The tunnel is
nearly 1800 feet long and about 6 feet in height throughout its length. At the south end of the tunnel was an
inscription of six lines which tells how the stone cutters,
who began at each end of the tunnel, could finally hear
each other as they approached the place where they were
to meet. The inscription stated that the tunnel was 1200
cubits long, indicating that the cubit was a measure
commonly used at that time. This inscription on the wall
of Hezekiah's tunnel was chiseled out by unauthorized
persons and is now preserved in the Museum at Con-
stantinople.[4] The author was amazed as he stood at the
place where the two parties of stone cutters met to see
how closely they had come together, and to notice how
the pick marks changed directions at the point of
completion.

Josiah

Josiah, the great-grandson of Hezekiah, was the most
remarkable monarch of Judah and the last righteous
ruler of the Southern Kingdom. Unlike his father and
grandfather he "did what was right in the eyes of the
Lord and walked in all the way of David his father, and
he did not turn aside to the right or to the left" (2 Kings
22:2). Josiah's religion and social reforms purged idolatry and paganism from the religion of the Southern
Kingdom. He restored the observance of the Passover,
brought about a spiritual awakening among his people,
and reestablished the worship of the one true God. During Josiah's reign, the power of Assyria began to wane;
Nineveh, its capital, was captured in 612 B.C. by the
Babylonians, who had begun their rise to prominence
in the world.

Josiah, opposing Egypt in a battle against Assyria, was
mortally wounded by Pharaoh Neco. The good king

died before he could reach Jerusalem. He was buried with extraordinary honors. His sons actually became vassals of Egypt; as such, they were not able to stand against Nebuchadnezzar, the Babylonian king, who swooped down on the defenseless Southern Kingdom.

Judah soon fell prey to Babylon. Jehoiakim, Jehoiachin, and Zedekiah, the last kings of Judah, surrendered to Nebuchadnezzar. Jehoiachin was taken to Babylon as a captive but given the privilege of eating at the Babylonian king's table. Zedekiah's eyes were put out, his sons were killed, and he too was carried to Babylon in chains. The most important and best educated of the people of the Southern Kingdom were taken into a Babylonian captivity which lasted nearly 50 years (587-539 B.C.), leaving only poor and untutored peasants living in Judah. Archeologists have uncovered clay tablets in Babylon which list the payments of oil, barley, and other foods that Jehoiachin and the Hebrew captives paid to Babylon.

During the era of the divided kingdoms, Palestine went through many years of political insecurity. To make matters worse, the Northern Kingdom and the Southern quarreled, bickered, and fought against each other. In spite of such troubles, though, there appears to have been some prosperity in the two nations. Both nations built excellent homes, better than those of their Canaanite neighbors. The Hebrew nations both imported commodities from abroad to improve their standard of living; the population increased. Conscripted military and labor groups were forced to build government projects, buildings, and cities. The hill country was placed under cultivation, and settled community became the order of the day. It seems that life was quite stable and comfortable for the Hebrews even during the years of the Divided Kingdom.

CHAPTER NINE

The Christian Era

The period of history covered by the New Testament lasted not even 100 years. This is so short a span that archeology cannot be expected to be as helpful as it has been in illuminating the centuries of Old Testament history. At best, archeology can give only a sketchy picture of the complex social, cultural, geographical, and political structure of Palestine as it existed under the influence of Greek culture and Roman rule during the ministry of Jesus. Nevertheless, the interesting Jewish traditions of this New Testament period provide a good deal of archeological evidence to verify the life, ministry, and mission of Jesus.

Up to the time of the Roman conquest in 63 B.C., the Israelites had known only a few years of independent nationhood under Saul, David, and Solomon. The most important influence on the Hebrews, as a result, was not statehood but their deeply rooted religious tradition. They never forgot the God of Abraham, Isaac, and Jacob. Idol worship, in the long run, was always abhorrent to the Israelites. They were closely united by having only the one temple in Jerusalem which served as the worship center for all Jews wherever they lived. All feasts had to be celebrated in Jerusalem and only there; this kept the people together as a unified religious body.

The Synagogue

The Jews, however, did have synagogues in their own communities and neighborhoods; the Talmud says that there were 480 in Jerusalem alone. The synagogue probably originated during the Babylonian captivity, when the Hebrews gathered together in little family groups to teach their children, read the Scriptures, and keep alive their faith in the midst of the Babylonian oppression. Ezra and Nehemiah seem to imply the use of synagogues during their time. The synagogue served as a teaching center for continuing the intricate laws, festivals, and customs of the Jewish religion. Worship was based mainly on the teaching of the law; no sacrifices were ever offered in the synagogues.

Greek Influences on Christianity

As early as the fifth century B.C. Greek culture began to have a great influence upon the Jews. During the Christian era Greek motifs were evident in the tombs, inscriptions, pottery, coinage, and writing used in Palestine. Herod the Great loved Greek culture, and he used Greek art forms and architectural designs in his building programs.

The greatest influence from the Greek world, though, came through the study and use of their language. The Jews were forced to learn Greek in order to trade in foreign markets; it became the language of the "learned." Because of the influence of Greece upon Palestine and

the rest of the known world, the New Testament was
written in Greek, one of the most expressive languages
in all the world. In addition, knowledge of Greek science
and philosophy aided the biblical writers in conveying
their faith to the Greek gentile world.

Archeological investigations during the latter part of
the 19th century unearthed thousands of letters, tax
papers, wills, and receipts in the dry sands of Egypt which
were written in the same type of Greek as was used by
the writers of the New Testament. It has become evident
that the "Good News" was recorded in an everyday language which was picturesque and flexible enough to
portray the message of salvation in Jesus. The language
of the New Testament was the everyday language of the
first century A.D. which was in use in most of the civilized
world of that day.

In 1871 archeologists discovered an interesting inscription in Jerusalem near the temple area. This inscription
contained seven lines written in Greek which warned
Gentiles to keep away from areas reserved for Jews only.
The inscription said, "No Gentile may enter inside the
enclosing screen around the temple. Whoever is caught
is alone responsible for the death which follows." Paul
was accused by the Jews of bringing Trophimus, a Gentile, into the temple; because of this, they attempted to
kill him (Acts 21:28).

Coinage Used in the Christian Era

About 60 years before the birth of Jesus, the Roman
armies entered Palestine and introduced Roman rule to
the land. Thus Rome added its influence to the life,
culture, customs, and manners of the Hebrews. Roman
coinage was introduced into Palestine by Pompey in
63 B.C. and continued for 100 years. Greek coinage also

continued to be used. The Jews themselves at times minted their own coins.

The New Testament refers to the coins of all three nations. Some of the Greek coins were the "talent" and the "pound" (also referred to as a "mina"). These were weights used in silver coinage, though gold talents and minas were also known at this time. The Greeks also had a silver "drachma" and "stater." The Romans used the "penny" or "denarius," the "farthing" and the "mite"; the silver "denarius" was the most familiar and the most common coinage of the New Testament. The Jews coined the "shekel" and "half-shekel" in silver, and other coins in bronze.

The symbols used by the Hebrews on their coins were palm trees, citrons, baskets, bundles of twigs, grapes, etc. They refused to use a graven image of a person, beast, or bird because of their abhorrence of idolatry and their reverence for the God of their ancestors. The Greeks and Romans, however, used the images of their rulers and kings, which makes it easy to date their coinage.

Coins have been very significant helps in dating the archeological sites in Palestine. When the excavation of a large building in Jericho was studied, the question of dating it came up. Coins found in the debris were helpful clues and enabled the archeologist to date the time when the site was occupied. The account of the decision follows:

> The earliest coins found were those of Herod I of which there were eleven. Twenty-seven bore the stamp of Archelaus; six were Herod Agrippa coins; and five were identified tentatively as belonging to one or another of the Procurators. Two of the Archelaus coins were found directly on major walls of the building. The presence of these forty-nine

coins, dating from the century covering the last
third of the first century B.C. and the first two-thirds
of the second century A.D. with the largest number
from the time of Archelaus at the mid-point of this
span, would seem to point to a major occupation at
the time of Christ and perhaps to the construction of
the building within this period.[1]

Coins were helpful in dating the Dead Sea Scrolls and
the ruins of the Monastery at Khirbet Qumran (see
Chapter 10). Most coins found in these caves and ruins
were dated from 4 B.C. to A.D. 68. Coins were discovered
from the reigns of Archelaus, Augustus, Tiberius, Agrippa, and Nero, all Roman rulers of Palestine during the
Christian era. The conclusion was reached that the monastery was constructed before 100 B.C. and was occupied
until 70 A.D.

Roman Roads

The Roman roads probably had the greatest influence
on the Holy Land. The city of Rome became the center
of civilization, with highways leading out to the far corners of the known world. The great Roman roads in
Palestine were probably not built until 70 A.D. It is
doubtful that Jesus ever walked on a Roman roadway,
but they were ready for his disciples to use as they
brought the Gospel to all parts of the Roman world.

These Roman thoroughfares were the finest ever to be
constructed by any nation until modern times. Fifteen
feet wide and three feet deep, they could be used for a
hundred years without repair. The first step in their
construction was to make a cut of the soil at the proper
width, then to remove the soil. The bottom of this cut
was packed and made solid by heavy rammers, then the
foundation of the road was laid with stones small enough
to be held by a human hand. The thickness of this layer

depended on the type of soil. When these rocks were packed into place, a nine-inch layer of coarse concrete made of lime and small stones was put in place over the foundation. Over this was laid a six-inch layer of finer concrete made of broken potsherds and lime. Upon this fine concrete was placed with great care a final layer of hard stones so carefully cut that no seam or fissure would admit water or jolt chariot wheels. Sometimes melted lead was poured in between the hand-cut stones to prevent water from coming into the fissures. Curb stones were laid along the side of the highway to form a shoulder. Sidewalks, foundations, and watering troughs were put in place along the curbs. These beautiful Roman thoroughfares were built in England, France, Italy, Greece, Asia Minor, Syria, and Palestine; some of them are still in use. The Appian Way outside the modern city of Rome stands today as a fine example of the skilled craftsmanship of the Roman road builders.

The general direction of the Roman roads in Palestine is well known today, thanks to archeology. Maps are now available which show the course of these highways. Inscriptions on milestones have been a great help in locating where these pavements were laid out. Caravan routes led from north to south and from east to west.

Tombs in the Christian Era

Tombs and graves from Roman times have provided a great deal of important architectural material to illuminate the origins of Christianity. Most Roman tombs were sealed and so remained intact through the centuries. In these unopened tombs the archeologist usually found coins, metal objects, pottery, and inscriptions. The larger tombs provided the burial space for a number of people; there were sometimes rooms lined with shelves on which were laid the "ossuaries" or limestone urns used in storing the dried and pulverized remains of bodies so as to allow room for the next generation to be buried in the same tomb. Often names were inscribed on these ossuaries, which provided a great deal of information about ancient names. On some of these ossuaries a cross had been inscribed, indicating that the person had been a Christian.

Pottery

Pottery, glassware, and metal objects are also very important for archeologists. The New Testament refers to many different household implements and furnishings, such as vessels, cups, pots, pans, platters, lamps, and dishes. Excavations in Palestine have discovered a great deal of pottery—some intact—as well as a huge amount of broken pieces called "potsherds."

Potters in Rome exported a type of red glazed pottery that was used extensively in the Holy Land. Each piece was stamped inside with the potter's own trademark. The shades and decorations are so well known that any site where this type of pottery is found can be dated.

Roman lamps were in use all over Palestine. Specialists who study these lamps can determine their age by the shape and by the material used. Patterns were often inscribed upon these lamps, such as leaves, flowers, fruit, and geometric designs. In the Christian era, the fish, lamb, grapes, and the cross were often used as art forms on lamps and their stands.

Various pieces of bronze ware have also been discovered. Bronze was used in making bowls, trays, jars, knives, shovels, and household ornaments. The form and type of bronze used has been helpful to the archeologists in dating their discoveries and sites.

Bethlehem and Jesus' Birth

Of all the New Testament sites which archeology has been able to determine positively, Bethlehem is probably the most interesting. The ancient site of this city stands on a ridge in the hill country of Judea, about six miles south of Jerusalem. This is the city of David's birth and boyhood; it later became the birthplace of the Son of David, Jesus. Here Ruth gleaned in the field of Boaz. David cared for his sheep in the hills surrounding Bethlehem.

It is generally assumed that Jesus was born about 4 B.C., since his birth occurred before the death of Herod the Great in that year. In the biblical accounts the birth took place in Bethlehem because of the decree of Caesar Augustus that all the world should be "enrolled." This forced Joseph and Mary to make the long tedious trip from Nazareth (Luke 2:1-3), for every family was required to return to its ancestral home.

Archeology has brought forth a number of papyrus documents attesting to the fact that a Roman census was taken every 14 years. Evidence has been found which points to a census taken shortly before the death of Herod the Great. Archeological discoveries have shown that Egypt, too, had periodic enrollments by households, conducted on a 14-year cycle. Actual census papers have been discovered in the sands of Egypt telling of these enrollments. An inscription discovered in Rome indicates that Cyrenius served as governor two times—once before the birth of Jesus and again shortly afterwards.

Justin, called "Martyr," who lived from 110 to 165 A.D., tells in his writings that Jesus was born in a cave in Bethlehem. A number of old houses in Bethlehem today are built over caves which are still used as stables for animals. The "Church of the Nativity" in Bethlehem, built by Emperor Constantine in 326 A.D., stands over a cave which people still venerate as the site of Jesus' birth. This Christian emperor cleared away the last trace of paganism in order to build his church over this cave. The "Church of the Nativity" underwent considerable rebuilding, especially in the sixth century, but the site of the original church is still there; it is the oldest Christian edifice still standing. One enters the cave by a series of steps leading down below the floor level to a grotto 33 feet long and 13 feet wide. Here Jesus was supposed to have been born, though we still lack clear evidence that this is the authentic birthplace of Jesus.[2] Nearby is the "Shepherds' Field," where the birth announcement was delivered in person by the angel. We have to be satisfied with the fact that somewhere near here Jesus was born.

The Inns

The inns of Palestine were located every 20 or 25 miles apart along the road. Bethlehem was about a day's journey from the region of the Dead Sea and would therefore have inns. These inns did not have private rooms as do modern-day motels. People and animals often slept together in one large room. The long, loose, flowing robes worn by these people served as blankets at night. The stable in Bethlehem would have offered much more privacy to a mother and newborn baby than an inn could possibly have done.

Herod the Great

Herod the Great played a very important part in the story of the birth of Jesus. He was an Edomite (a descendant of Esau), related to the Hebrews, and a Jew by religion but not in practice. The greater part of the territory of the Kingdoms of Israel and Judah had been put under his control. He is remembered for two things: his building programs and his brutality. He put to death his own mother and wife; he had his brother-in-law forcibly drowned in a swimming pool and ordered several of his own sons strangled. Before Herod died he issued a command that a large number of the leading Jews of Palestine be gathered together and executed at the time of his death in order that there might be a great deal of mourning in Judea for him. This order, however, was not carried out. It would not be surprising for such a suspicious and insecure Roman ruler to order the brutal massacre of the infants of Bethlehem in order to destroy Mary's child, who had so recently been visited by the wise men from the East.

Most of the Jews hated Herod and always considered him a usurper to the throne of David. Some of the younger Jews, however, formed a distinct party known as the Herodians. This group was partly religious, partly political, and partly cultural, loving the luxury of Roman dress and society. The members of the Herodian Party were a real offense to the loyal Hebrews, yet even they were willing to cooperate with the Pharisees against Jesus (Mark 3:6; 12:13).

Despite his cruelty, Herod the Great was also the great builder who prepared the way for Jesus. He beautified and enlarged the cities where Jesus and his disciples were to visit and carry out their evangelization of the people, and he probably spent more time in building up the city of Jerusalem than any of the other sites in Palestine. He reinforced the northern wall of the city, before his time the only part of the wall susceptible to attack. On this wall he constructed three huge defensive towers, using solid masonry, to make the city impregnable. To the south of this fort he built a magnificent palace surrounded by groves of trees and canals.

The Castle Antonia

Near the temple Herod the Great constructed a great fortress and named it Antonia in honor of Mark Anthony. This fort was built on a precipice about 75 feet in height. Four strong towers on the corners were constructed for further defense. The fortress was well equipped, and a Roman cohort was always stationed there to discourage uprisings by the Jews. Archeological evidence from this site reveals patterns scratched on the surface of the large stones used as the pavement, the relics of a gambling game played by soldiers on duty at the citadel. It was to this structure that Paul was taken for safekeeping when attacked by the Jews; some even think that Jesus was taken there for his trial before Pilate.

Herod Enlarges the Temple

Herod's greatest building activity, though, was enlarging the temple built by Zerubbabel in the post-exilic period. He lavished huge sums on the great worship center, making it worthy of its fame as the place of worship for Jews from all over the world. He adorned it with splendid colonnaded courts and porches. He had a thousand Hebrew priests trained in carpentry and masonry so that they alone might enter the temple and not desecrate the building during its remodeling. The temple was rebuilt on its own original foundation. The front walls were ornamented with gold plate, as was the roof. The building was described as "a snowy mountain covered with gold." When Herod's temple was completed it rose 200 feet above the Brook Kedron.

Herod Builds

A part of the retaining wall which held up the temple and its courts still remains in the city. These stones were cut by the workmen of King Herod and consist of stone blocks carefully hewn and fitted together, forming the famous "wailing wall" where 14 rows of Herodian masonry can be seen today at ground level.[3]

Herod the Great is also remembered for building the seaport city of Caesarea, midway on the coast between Mount Carmel and Joppa. He spent 12 years making Caesarea one of the most beautiful and important sites in Palestine. From 6 to 66 A.D. Caesarea became the seat of the Roman government in Palestine. Remains of a stadium, an amphitheater, a market place, and a temple have been found. In 1961 an Italian archeological expedition in Caesarea found the name "Pontius Pilate" inscribed on a stone slab 24 inches long and 30 inches wide; the name of the Roman Emperor Tiberius was inscribed on the same stone. Jesus apparently never visited Caesarea, but the Roman city was important in the ministry of Peter, Philip, Paul, and Cornelius. Paul was tried before Festus and Herod Agrippa in this city (Acts 25:23-27).

Jericho

The city of Jericho which Jesus knew was a far cry from the city Joshua conquered as he led the Israelites into the promised land. Under the prosperity of the Herods, Jericho became a mecca for the wealthy Hebrews and Romans. Its very favorable climate made it a desirable place for winter living. King Herod erected a magnificent winter palace here. He also built a citadel, a theater, and an amphitheater. It was at Jericho that Jesus healed blind Bartimaeus.

Sebaste

The once proud capital of the Northern Kingdom, Samaria, which had been destroyed by the Assyrians in 721, was rebuilt by Herod the Great. The city was renamed Sebaste, the Greek form of the title Augustus, who was then ruler of the Roman Empire. Herod sent 6,000 of his war veterans to occupy the city. Herod also erected a magnificent worship center on the ruin of Jezebel's pagan temple of eight centuries earlier. The structure was almost 225 feet square and was built in honor of Caesar Augustus of Rome. Excavations have shown that a massive stairway led to the temple. East of this magnificent building a great forum was constructed, which contained a large open square surrounded by shops. A large stadium was built at the edge of the valley north of the temple. The stadium was approximately 530 feet long and 190 feet wide and was used as a sports arena.[4]

The Herodium

Herod the Great built a great stronghold, called the "Herodium," three miles south of Bethlehem. The hill on which this fort was built was raised until it became the highest point in the area. Access to this stronghold was gained solely by a long staircase of 200 polished stone steps. The fortress was protected by four circular towers from which there was a magnificent view of the entire countryside. Within the Herodium itself were lavish and sumptuous apartments. Here Herod lived occasionally. Ruins of the surrounding wall still stand, together with cisterns, pools, and fountains. The surrounding plains were dotted with villas and palaces of his courtiers. Herod the Great planned that this fortress should become the mausoleum in which he was to be buried.[5]

Herod's Death

Herod the Great died of dropsy, gangrene, and other loathsome diseases. In full royal regalia, the funeral procession of the dead king marched from Jericho to the Herodium at Bethlehem. Herod's body lay on a golden, gem-encrusted bier, beneath a great purple pall. His golden crown was on his head, and his scepter was placed in his right hand. Those members of his own family that he had not murdered followed the bier. Then came the Royal Guard, the Thracian Regiment, the German Regiment, the Galatian Regiment, and the Regiments of the Line in full battle array. This imposing procession was followed by 500 servants carrying spices to be placed in the tomb at the Herodium.

In the Jewish-Roman War in 66 A.D. the Herodium was destroyed, and only the ruins remain today. The present site is called Frank Mountain.[6]

Nazareth

The death of Herod the Great was the signal for Joseph and Mary to return from Egypt with Jesus. They did not take the little boy Jesus back to Bethlehem, though, for Archelaus, the worst of Herod's sons, then ruled Judea. Instead, they went to Nazareth, where in their humble home they cared for the child.

The site of Nazareth, secluded as it was among the surrounding hills, was one of the most peaceful locations in all Palestine. No caravan route ever passed through Jesus' boyhood home. The scenery was expansive, if not breath-taking. Until very recently the social life of Nazareth had not changed a great deal since the days of Jesus.

At the foot of one of the many hills that surround

Nazareth is a fountain, the only source of water in the immediate vicinity. Mary probably took the boy Jesus with her many times to the well as she secured the drinking water for her family. Today the Greek Church of the Annunciation is built over the well, from which water is piped down the hill to Mary's spring. It is still used as a source of water for the people of Nazareth.[7]

There is no archeological evidence to indicate that Nazareth existed before 600 B.C.; as a result, the city is not mentioned in the Old Testament. The Nazareth synagogue of Jesus' day was completely destroyed; its exact site cannot be determined today.

Capernaum

The city of Capernaum, lying on the northwestern shores of the Sea of Galilee, was a bustling fishing port. Capernaum was apparently a Roman military post, since it was there that the God-fearing Roman centurion asked Jesus to heal his servant (Matt. 8:5-13). Jesus preached in a synagogue in Capernaum; however, the site of this building has not yet been discovered by archeologists. Several synagogues in the area have been uncovered which were similar to the one Jesus preached in, but they were probably built in 70-200 A.D. One of Jesus' disciples was Matthew, the tax collector, whose office was at Capernaum (Matt. 9:9).

Tax Collectors

Several documents have been discovered which reveal the true character of the tax collectors of Jesus' day: They earned their living by the extortion of tax money. Matthew and Zacchaeus, then, must have been looked down upon by the people before their conversion. Other documents indicate that a heavy duty was placed on all exports and imports of every kind. Land, homes, flocks, furnishings, and food were all taxed up to twenty per cent. All important cities and trade routes were well supplied with government tax collectors. It seems likely that a great many Jews in Palestine made their livelihood by collecting taxes from their own people for the hated Roman government.[8]

Caesarea Philippi

At Caesarea Philippi, nearly 50 miles north of Galilee, Peter made his great confession: "You are the Christ, the Son of the living God" (Matt. 16:16). This was the climax of Jesus' ministry with his disciples. Now Christ was ready for the long trek to Jerusalem, where quickly began the events that led to his betrayal, trials, crucifixion, and death.

Pentecost

After the ascension of Jesus (Acts 1:9) the disciples returned to Jerusalem to await the promised outpouring of the Holy Spirit. During this 10-day waiting period they decided to fill the vacancy left by the death of Judas Iscariot. Matthias was chosen by lot for this replacement. Then, after a gathering of 10 days in prayer in the upper room in Jerusalem, the Holy Spirit came in an awesome and powerful way (Acts 1:13-26).

The day fell on the Old Testament celebration of Pentecost, or the "Feast of Weeks," as it was often called. This Old Testament festival always came 50 days after the Passover. For this observance the Jews presented to the Lord two loaves of bread, along with an offering of lambs and other animals (Lev. 23:18); the celebration was actually a dedication of their crops to the Lord before they used the produce for themselves. This festival had lately come to be also a commemoration of their release from bondage in Egypt (Deut. 16:9-12).

The New Testament Day of Pentecost came 50 days after the resurrection of Jesus, or 10 days after his ascension. The Holy Spirit came in a special way to empower the disciples for their ministry. Three thousand people were baptized in Jerusalem, marking the occasion as the birthday of the church (Acts 2:14).

Among the people who heard the disciples speaking in strange tongues were Jews from Parthia, Media, Elim, Phrygia, Libya, Crete, Rome, Arabia, and many other countries. Archeological evidence reveals that there were Jews living in all these lands in the New Testament era. Archeological remains of a little Jewish colony called Samaria in Egypt were discovered in a large oasis about 40 miles south and west of Cairo. Some of these Jews were bankers, police officers, merchants, and tax collectors. Nearly one-fourth of the great city of Alexandria was at that time a Jewish district.[9]

Some of these Hebrews became wealthy and influential merchants. In some cases they had spent so much time outside of Palestine that they had even forgotten the Hebrew language. The "speaking in tongues" proved to be a Christian witness for these Jews who had returned to Palestine for their retirement; the testimony to the Holy Spirit's power was proclaimed to them in their adopted languages.

Tiberias

Tiberias, built on the western shore of the Sea of Galilee, was used by Herod Antipas, son of Herod the Great, as his new capital. The city was probably founded in 18 A.D., and its name was often applied to the Sea itself, indicating the importance of Tiberias. Very few

Jews ever lived in this Roman city, because Herod Antipas had removed many Jewish graves in order to make room for his new city. According to the Scriptures, Jesus apparently never visited the city.

Archeology has not given us much information about the actual life and ministry of Jesus. The actual sites of Jesus' birthplace, his boyhood home, his robe, his cross, the place of his crucifixion, and the tomb in which his body was placed are all hidden to us. This is not really very important, though, for we as Christians should seek to know the risen living Savior instead of just the sites which he hallowed by his physical presence. Nevertheless, the hills of Bethlehem, the cliffs of Nazareth, the shores of Galilee, and the Mount of Olives still remain as mute reminders of the earthly life of God's Son, the long-awaited Savior who "came not to be served but to serve, and to give his life as a ransom for many" (Mark 10:45).

The Dead Sea Scrolls

One day in 1947 a 15-year-old Bedouin boy named Muhammed the Wolf was pasturing his flock of goats by the wild, craggy, desolate foothills on the northwest shore of the Dead Sea. One of his shaggy goats had chanced to stray from the rest of the flock. While searching for this aggravating animal, the boy noticed a small circular hole in the rocky cliffs. His curiosity got the better of him, so he crawled up the steep cliff to look more closely. At first he could see nothing but an open cave. Muhammed picked up a stone and threw it into the cave; he was startled to hear a strange, echoing sound of shattering pottery instead of the dull thud of a stone on the bottom of the hollow cave. Still apprehensive, he went to find a friend to go with him to examine his discovery. Braving the terrors of an unexplored cave, they climbed into the opening and found themselves in a narrow cleft of rock.[1]

To their amazement, the boys discovered that there was a large number of dust-covered pottery jars standing on the floor of the cave. One of these jars had been shattered by the stone that Muhammed had hurled through the opening. The boys had hoped to find a hidden treasure of gold and silver, but instead they discovered that the jars contained rolls of papyrus, leather, and metal covered with writing, all carefully wrapped in cloth. Disgusted at not finding buried treasure, the two boys picked out the best looking rolls and jars, stuffing them in the bosom of their long flowing robes, climbed back down the steep precipice, and hurried off to smuggle them into Bethlehem, where they hoped to sell them for a few piasters.

One of the merchants to whom the boys tried to sell the scrolls became excited about the discovery and informed the Metropolitan (or head) of the Orthodox Monastery of St. Mark in Old Jerusalem. The Metropolitan recognized that the writing on the scrolls was in Hebrew, but he was not able to determine the importance of the scrolls. He purchased five of them. Not satisfied with his purchase, he made a special attempt to find all the manuscripts which had been removed from the cave, but had to be content with these five. Realizing that they might be very important documents, he sought professional help from the French School of Biblical and Archeological Studies in Old Jerusalem. A visiting Dutch professor of archeology at the school examined the scrolls, which were 23 feet long, and identified them as a very old copy of Isaiah.[2] It soon became the most famous of all the scrolls.

The Metropolitan sent his scrolls to the United States for safekeeping, since the bitter struggle for the partitioning of Palestine was at white heat; the monastery had already been damaged in the bombings of Old Jerusalem. The Jordanian government, however, insisted that the scrolls be returned to Jordan at once, since all archeological discoveries in Jordan belonged, by law, to that nation.

Professor E. L. Sukenik of the Hebrew University of Jerusalem purchased some of the scrolls that had been brought to Bethlehem by the two Bedouin boys; as he studied them, he became increasingly convinced of their antiquity and significance. He declared, "It may be that this is one of the greatest finds ever made in Palestine." [3] Professor W. F. Albright, archeologist of Johns Hopkins University in Baltimore, Md., after examining photographs of the scrolls, wrote, "My heartiest congratulations on the greatest manuscript discovery of modern times." [4]

Mr. G. L. Harding, in charge of the Department of Antiquities of Jordan (1936-1956), organized a search party to discover the precise location of the cave where the scrolls had been discovered. No one seemed to know anything of its location. Finally, Mr. Harding obtained from the Jordanian government a detachment of troops to help search the area west of the Dead Sea.

Finally, after a delay of nearly two years, the original cave was discovered near the Wadi Qumran on February 15, 1949. Mr. Harding and his assistants began a systematic archeological examination of the cave. His crew of workers were amazed at the number of fragments of leather and linen wrappings from which the contents had been removed. Broken pieces of pottery lay strewed everywhere as the mute evidence of the protection they had once afforded this ancient library. It was quite obvious that the cave had been looted many times since Muhammed had first entered its mouth. The Bedouin tribesmen were well aware of the monetary value of these old documents and were willing to sell their loot to anyone at their own price. Mr. Harding won the confidence of the Bedouins and was able to recover some 600 manuscript fragments representing various literary works.[5]

These manuscript fragments contained parts of nearly every book in the Old Testament. Perhaps the most valuable find was the Isaiah scroll, which was 23 feet long and nearly 10 inches high. This scroll contained nearly all of Isaiah. Another important manuscript was the Habakkuk commentary, which was four and one-half feet long and less than six inches wide. This scroll contained chapter one and two of Habakkuk plus a free running commentary on the two chapters. Another important scroll contained several chapters of Genesis. This manuscript was 9 feet long and 12 inches wide. An interesting document called "The War of the Sons of Light with the Sons of Darkness" was also found in this ancient library. A "Manual of Discipline," measuring six feet in length and nine inches wide, contained the rules and regulations of a religious sect known as the Essenes. Another fragment contained a "Thanksgiving Psalm." Portions of Daniel, Exodus, Leviticus, Numbers, Deuteronomy, Ruth, Psalms, and Jeremiah were included in the fragments found in this first cave.[6]

Professor Sukenik reported that none of the scrolls were dated after 70 A.D. Thus, in one blow, the textual evidence for the Old Testament had been advanced at least a thousand years, since the previous standard texts for the Hebrew Bible came from sources dating from 800 to 900 A.D.

The linen cloth wrappings which protected the manuscripts were studied, and it was decided that the scrolls had each been carefully wrapped in cloth woven on the looms of Palestine. The matching pieces of pottery were glued together, and it was then ascertained that the original jars were cylindrical in shape and stood about 26 inches high. The cloth-wrapped scrolls had been carefully placed inside the jars.

The potsherds, lying in great quantity at the bottom of the cave, were dated according to three types of evidence. First, the style of writing represented a period of 300 years between the third century B.C. and the middle of the first century A.D. Linguists have agreed with the truth of these studies. Second, the linen in which the scrolls were wrapped was proved by the carbon 14 test to belong to the general period of 175 B.C. to 225 A.D. Finally, a study of the pottery in the cave was ascertained as having been made during the end of the Greek period, in the first century B.C., while some of the potsherds were dated in the Roman period of the second century A.D. It was quite definitely established that the scrolls were placed in the cave sometime during the period of time from 150 B.C. to 100 A.D. Several fragments of two clay lamps and a cooking pot from the first century were also discovered in this cave.

Khirbet Qumran

This amazing discovery began much speculation about the source of this ancient library. Archeologists soon linked the library to some ruins, long known as Khirbet Qumran, which were situated on a plateau just north of Wadi Qumran. The ruins of this little settlement on the shores of the Dead Sea lay about eight miles south of Jericho. Both the site and the cave appeared to be from the first and second centuries A.D. Jars identical to those found in the caves were discovered in the ruins of Khirbet Qumran. Identical coins and Roman lamps were also unearthed in both places.

Archeologists agreed that during the first century, Khirbat Qumran was the flourishing monastery of an ascetic Jewish sect called the Essenes. The Essenes appear to have founded this community about 140 B.C.

The ruins of this settlement included rooms for preparing and eating food. There were smelters for metal work, desks for copying sacred books, cisterns for storing water, rooms for assembly and worship, ovens for baking bread, and bins for storing grain. The quality of the building was very poor, and its construction was inferior. Probably the Essenes did not have any architects or masons in the group. Most of information regarding this religious sect of the pre-Christian and Christian era has come to us from three authors of the first century A.D.: Pliny, Philo, and Josephus.[7]

Pliny

Foremost of these authors was Pliny, who in his *Natural History* describes the Essene village in this way: "On the west side of the Dead Sea, but out of range of the noxious exhalations of the coast, is the solitary tribe of the Essenes, which is remarkable beyond all the other tribes in the whole world, as it has no women and has renounced all sexual desire, has no money, and has only palm-trees for company. Day by day the throng of refugees is recruited to an equal number by numerous accessions of persons tired of life and driven thither by the waves of fortune to adopt their manners. Thus through thousands of ages (incredible to relate) a race in which no one is born lives on for ever: so prolific for their advantage is other men's weariness of life!

"Lying below the Essenes was formerly the town of Engedi, second only to Jerusalem in the fertility of its land and in its groves of palm-trees, but now like Jerusalem a heap of ashes. Next comes Masada, a fortress on a rock, itself also not far from the Dead Sea. This is the limit of Judea." [8]

Here Pliny is evidently describing the people who inhabited Khirbet Qumran, those men who, during a siege hid the monastery library in the caves at Wadi Qumran.

Philo

Philo, an Alexandrian Hebrew (20 B.C.-50 A.D.), gives further information about the Essenes in a rather lengthy work entitled "Every Good Man Is Free." He writes:

> Palestinian Syria, too, has not failed to produce high moral excellence. In this country live a considerable part of the very populous nation of the Jews, including, as it is said, certain persons, more than four thousand in number, called Essenes. Their name, which is, I think, a variation, though the form of the Greek is inexact, of *hosiotes* (holiness), is given them, because they have shown themselves especially devout in the service of God, not by offering sacrifices of animals, but by resolving to sanctify their minds. The first thing about these people is that they live in villages and avoid the cities because of the iniquities which have become inveterate among city dwellers, for they know that their company would have a deadly effect upon their own souls, like a disease brought by a pestilential atmosphere. Some of them labour on the land and others pursue such crafts as co-operate with peace and so benefit themselves and their neighbours. They do not hoard gold and silver or acquire great slices of land because they desire the revenues therefrom, but provide what is needed for the necessary requirements of life. For while they stand almost alone in the whole of mankind in that they have become moneyless and landless by deliberate action rather than by lack of good fortune, they are esteemed exceedingly rich, because they judge frugality with contentment to be, as indeed it is, an abundance of wealth. As for darts, javelins, daggers, or the helmet, breast-plate or shield, you could not find a single manufacturer of them, nor,

in general, any person making weapons or engines or plying any industry connected with war, nor indeed, any of the peaceful kind, which easily lapse into vice, for they have not the vaguest idea of commerce either wholesale or retail or marine, but pack the inducements to covetousness off in disgrace. Not a single slave is to be found amongst them, but all are free exchanging services with each other, and they denounce the owners of slaves. They are trained in piety, holiness, justice, domestic and civil conduct, knowledge of what is truly good, or evil, or indifferent, and how to choose what they should and avoid the opposite, taking for their defining standards these three, love of God, love of virtue, love of men. Their love of God they show by a multitude of proofs, by religious purity constant and unbroken throughout their lives, by abstinence from oaths, by veracity, by their belief that the Godhead is the cause of all good things and nothing bad; their love of virtue, by their freedom from the love of either money or reputation or pleasure, by self-mastery and endurance again by frugality, simple living, contentment, humility, respect for law, steadiness and all similar qualities; their love of men by benevolence and sense of equality, and their spirit of fellowship, which defies description, though a few words on it will not be out of place. First of all then, no one's house is his own in the sense that it is not shared by all, for besides the fact that they dwell together in communities, the door is open to visitors from elsewhere who share their convictions.

Again they all have a single treasury and common disbursements; their clothes are held in common and also their food through their institution of public meals. In no other community can we find the custom of sharing roof, life and board more firmly established in actual practice. And that is no more than one would expect. For all the wages which they earn in the day's work they do not keep as their private property, but throw them into the common

stock and allow the benefit thus accruing to be
shared by those who wish to use it. The sick are not
neglected because they cannot provide anything, but
have the cost of their treatment lying ready in the
common stock, so that they can meet expenses out of
the greater wealth in full security. To the elder men
too is given the respect and care which real children
give to their parents, and they receive from countless
hands and minds a full and generous maintenance for
their latter years.[9]

Josephus

Josephus, a Jewish historian (37-95 A.D.), includes an
account of the Essenes in his second book called *Antiquities of the Jews.*

The doctrine of the Essenes is this: That all things
are best ascribed to God. They teach the immortality
of souls, and esteem that the rewards of righteousness are to be earnestly striven for: and when they
send what they have dedicated to God into the temple they do not offer sacrifices, because they have
more pure lustrations of their own; on which account they are excluded from the common court of
the temple, but offer their sacrifices themselves; yet
is their course of life better than that of other men;
and they entirely addict themselves to husbandry.
It also deserves our admiration, how much they ex-
ceed all other men that addict themselves to virtue,
and this in righteousness; and indeed to such a degree, that as it hath never appeared among any
other men . . . so hath it endured a long time among
them. This is demonstrated by that institution of
theirs, which will not suffer any thing to hinder them
from having all things in common; so that a rich
man enjoys no more of his own wealth than he who
hath nothing at all.

There are about 4000 men that live in this way,
and neither marry wives, nor are desirous to keep servants; as thinking the latter tempts men to be unjust,

and the former gives the handle to domestic quarrels; but as they live by themselves, they minister one
to another. They also appoint stewards to receive the
incomes of their revenues, and of the fruits of the
ground; such as are good men and priest, who are to
get their corn and their food ready for them. They
none of them differ from others of the Essenes in
their way of living.[10]

The Monastery Plan

Archeologists exploring the ruins of the ancient Essene
monastery at Khirbet Qumran have discovered that the
main building was 100 feet wide and 200 feet long; this
was the center of the monastery of the Essenes. In the
northwest corner of this structure was an immense tower
with a thick stone wall, reinforced by stone embank-
ments. The kitchen appears to be east of the tower, since
evidences of several fireplaces were found here. A dining
room was nearby; near the dining room was a pantry in
which were stacked nearly a thousand bowls. Southeast of
the tower was an assembly hall with plastered benches
suggesting a meeting place. Alongside this room was a
writing room with tables, pens, and inkwells. One of
the inkwells actually had some dried ink remaining in it.
It seems that manuscripts were copied here by the Essene
scribes. In the southeastern part of the building were
two cisterns; these were carefully constructed and plastered in order to hold water. Thirty other cisterns were
discovered in the vicinity of this arid-desert monastery.
A cemetery located near the monastery contained nearly
a thousand graves.

Under Threat of War

Evidently, the Dead Sea Scrolls appear to have been
hurriedly placed in the jars by the community at Khirbet
Qumran and stored in these caves to be preserved because

of some forthcoming catastrophe. The caves were not very safe and did erode; in several cases, a part of the roof fell in. The caves presented a physical condition hardly conducive for preserving the scrolls permanently, so it has been assumed that the scrolls were placed there temporarily under the threat of war, invasion, or attack. Something must have happened to the members of the Essene sect who hid these scrolls, for they never returned to pick up the hidden library. Possibly they were victims of the Romans in their final attempt to sack Jerusalem in 66 A.D.; perhaps they were carried away as prisoners, never to return. In any case, the site was totally abandoned, and it remained so until the discovery by young Muhammed in 1947.

Wadi Murabba'at

In October 1951 another cave, located about 11 miles to the south of Wadi Qumran, was discovered by money-conscious Bedouins. This cave was called Wadi Murabba'at. Later, four other caves were found near the same almost vertical rockface. By the time an official party arrived at Wadi Murabba'at to conduct an examination, 34 Bedouins were busily engaged in plundering these five new archeological discoveries. To satisfy these cave explorers, several of them were employed in the archeological expedition.

The caves penetrated deep into the rocks for a considerable distance. Layers of dust covered everything. Erosion had taken its toll. The roofs of two of these caves were weakened to the condition of being extremely dangerous, having already sunk in certain places.

The caves have been inhabited by many different periods of history, but the most interesting finds were from the Roman period. A number of coins belonging to the period from 132 to 135 A.D. dated these caves accurately as belonging to the early Christian era. Some of the potsherds were inscribed in Greek or Hebrew. Several papyri written in Hebrew were found. Other potsherds, pieces of metal, wooden objects, leather fragments, and scraps of cloth indicated that the last people to occupy the caves came from the second century B.C.

Among the documents discovered in these caves were fragments of several books of the Bible, including Genesis, Numbers, and the Psalms. A fragment from the Minor Prophets, written in uncial script on leather, could be traced to the first century B.C. Other scrolls containing parts of Micah, Jonah, Nahum, Habakkuk, Zephaniah, and Zechariah were found in these caves. Another manuscript containing parts of the Old Testament from the middle of Joel to the end of Zephaniah was also found here.[11]

One of the most interesting discoveries connected with the Dead Sea Scrolls was that earthen jars were used in storing them. Jars of this kind had been in use for many years for storing a wide variety of commodities prior to the Christian era. This process probably began in Egypt when the embalmers placed the vital organs of the body in jars beside the mummy at burial. Thus it became customary in the Orient to store strange and valuable commodities in clay pots. Jeremiah speaks of this, "Thus says the Lord of hosts, the God of Israel: Take these deeds, both this sealed deed of purchase and this open deed, and put them in an earthenware vessel, that they may last for a long time" (Jer. 32:14). Literary compositions were placed in jars and sealed with pitch to preserve them for posterity.

The state of Israel purchased the scrolls which had been sent to the United States, and has recently housed the scrolls from the first cave in a new museum, called

"The Shrine of the Book." After years of separation, the documents from the Qumran community have once again been brought together into a place where all may come to see with their own eyes how the archeologist's work has made the saving history of the past alive and real today.

GLOSSARY

Amarna tablets	clay tablets discovered at Amarna, 190 miles south of Cairo, containing correspondence between the Pharaohs of Egypt and the kings of Asia, Syria, and Palestine.
Ammonites	According to Gen. 19:38 the descendants of Lot's incestuous relation with his younger daughter, who lived east of the Jordan River.
Archeology	study of old or ancient things left behind by men during the past ages.
Artifact	a tool, utensil, implement, or piece of furniture made by man and studied by an archeologist to reconstruct history.
Baal	a nature diety; the chief pagan god worshiped by the Canaanites at the time of Israel's entrance into the Promised Land.
Black obelisk of Shalmaneser III	a limestone pillar erected near Shalmaneser's palace to commemorate the first thirty-one years of his reign, c. 850 B.C.
Canopic jars	large vases used in Egypt for preserving the heart and intestines of dead people before mummification.
Carbon 14 test	a means af dating organic matter discovered in archeology by the principle that all living things absorb from the atmosphere a radioactive form of carbon. This carbon slowly diminishes at a known rate, thus making it possible to determine the age of ancient organic matter.

Hammurabi   King of Babylon who inscribed his famous laws on a pillar of black diorite stone nearly eight feet high about 1723 B.C.

Codex   a manuscript volume of an ancient copy of the Scriptures.

Craniometer   an instrument for measuring the external dimensions of a skull.

Cuneiform   a system of writing which used wedge-shaped characters forced into soft clay or stone; used in Egypt, Persia, and Assyria.

Cursive   a writing style using flowing strokes with letters joined together.

Edomites   in the Bible, the descendants of Esau, the brother of Jacob, who lived south of the Dead Sea.

Essenes   an ascetic celibate brotherhood of Jews living since the second century B.C. which spent its time in study of the Torah. The Dead Sea Scrolls were part of their library.

Fossil   any remains, impression, or trace of an animal or plant found in rock, coal, or mineral.

Herodians   a political party of Jewish people who sought the political favor of King Herod.

Hittite   a powerful ancient civilization which lived in Asia Minor c. 1900-1200 B.C. They pushed their way into Syria and Canaan many times.

Hivites   in the Bible, the descendants of Canaan, son of Ham, who lived near Tyre and Sidon.

Hieroglyphics   an Egyptian writing system using pictures of the thing named by the words for which the symbols stand.

Hyksos   a Semitic people of Canaan which infiltrated Egypt for a long time and eventually became powerful enough to rule Egypt from the 18th to the 16th centuries B.C.

Khirbet Qumran   an old ruin of a monastery of Essenes near the Dead Sea which gives interesting insight into this sect. Produced and hid the Dead Sea Scrolls.

Mari tablets	twenty thousand clay tablets found in the ruins of the King's Palace at Mari on the Euphrates River, containing records parallel to the patriarchal records of Genesis.
Midianites	descendants of Midian, a son of Abraham, who lived in and near the peninsula of Sinai. Moses married a daughter of the priest of Midian.
Moabites	descendants of Lot's incestuous relation with his oldest daughter, who lived east of the Dead Sea (Gen. 38).
Moabite stone	a slab of black basalt stone three feet ten inches high, two feet wide, and ten and one-half inches thick found in the Moabite capital, Dibon. It contains inscriptions referring to the Hebrews.
Natron	a mineral, hydrated sodium carbonate, used by the Egyptians to mummify a body.
Nomad	a people without a fixed abode, traveling from place to place to find pasture and food.
Nuzi tablets	clay tablets discovered near Nineveh which contain many laws and customs similar to those of the patriarchs.
Obelisk	a tapering, four-sided shaft of stone, used as an ancient monument and often containing valuable inscriptions.
Ossuary	a box, urn, or container in which are stored the bones of the dead.
Papyrus	a writing material made in Egypt from a tall plant. The thin strips of the pith are laid together, soaked, pressed, and dried.
Philistines	a group of non-Semitic people who settled on the coast of Palestine about 1200 B.C. They constantly plagued the Israelites.
Ras Shamra tablets	clay tablets discovered at Ugarit in Northern Syria, opposite the island of Cyprus. Most of these tablets are poems about Canaanite gods and pagan worship. Many of the customs expressed are similar to those of the Hebrews.
Renaissance	a period of great revival in learning during the 14th, 15th, and 16th centuries in Europe marking the transition from the medieval to the modern world.

Rosetta stone   a stone found in Rosetta, Egypt, containing inscriptions in three different languages. It proved to be the key to deciphering several ancient languages.

Sarcophagus   a stone coffin, bearing inscriptions and often used as a monument.

Semites   the descendants of Shem, son of Noah.

Stele   an upright slab of stone or pillar bearing an inscription.

Stratification   the layers of civilization at a once inhabited site discovered by archeology. Most cities were built on top of a destroyed city. In many cases the old stones were reused. In this way from ten to twenty cities were often built on one site.

Tell   an Arabic word for "hill" used to designate the mound which was occupied by a succession of cities and towns.

Teraphim   statuettes of pagan gods or deities.

Uncial   a form of writing in which all the letters were capitalized and written the same height.

Wadi   a channel of a watercourse which is dry except during periods of rainfall.

Wadi Murabba'at   four large caves were found in this Wadi near Khirbet Qumran which contained many valuable scrolls and fragments of the Scriptures.

Wadi Qumran   a more exact designation of the site of the cave near which the first of the Dead Sea Scrolls were discovered. It lies about seven miles from Jericho.

Ziggurat   a pagan temple in the form of a series of graduated pyramids or stories; the top story is attained by a series of steps.

NOTES

Chapter One: Introduction to Archeology

1. MERRILL F. UNGER, *Archeology and the Old Testament* (Grand Rapids, Mich.: Zondervan, 1954), pp. 19-20.
2. CHARLES F. PFEIFFER, *The Biblical World* (Grand Rapids, Mich.: Baker Book House, 1966), pp. 143-144.
3. JACK FINNEGAN, *Light from the Ancient Past* (Princeton, N.J.: Princeton University Press, 1959, rev. ed.) , p. 112.
4. *Ibid.,* pp. 395-397.
5. WILLIAM F. ALBRIGHT, *Archeology and the Religion of Israel* (Baltimore: Johns Hopkins Press, 1941), p. 176.

Chapter Two: The Techniques of Archeology

Chapter Three: The Patriarchs

1. JOSEPH P. FREE, *Archaeology and Bible History* (Wheaton, Ill.: Van Kampen Press, 1950), p. 49.
2. *Ibid.,* pp. 49, 50.
3. PFEIFFER, *op. cit.,* pp. 66-67.
4. CYRUS H. GORDON, *The World of the Old Testament* (Garden City, N.Y.: Doubleday, 1958), pp. 81-82.
5. FINNEGAN, *op. cit.,* pp. 66-67.
6. FREE, *op. cit.,* pp. 54-55.
7. *Ibid.,* pp. 55-56.
8. *Ibid.,* p. 56.
9. FINNEGAN, *op. cit.,* pp. 65-67.
10. UNGER, *Archeology and the Old Testament,* p. 123.
11. FINNEGAN, *op. cit.,* p. 67.
12. FREE, *op. cit.,* p. 230.

Chapter Four: The Exodus from Egypt

1. FINNEGAN, *op. cit.,* pp. 94-95.

2. MILLAR BURROWS, *What Mean These Stones* (New Haven: American Schools of Oriental Research, 1944), p. 71.

3. FREE, *op. cit.,* p. 85.

4. FINNEGAN, *op. cit.,* p. 100.

5. G. ERNEST WRIGHT and FLOYD FILSON, *The Westminster Historical Atlas to the Bible* (Philadelphia: Westminster, 1945), p. 37.

6. FLOYD E. HAMILTON, *The Basis of Christian Belief* (New York: Harper, 1946), p. 172.

7. FREE, *op. cit.,* p. 101.

8. FINNEGAN, *op. cit.,* p. 151.

9. *Ibid.,* pp. 58-62.

Chapter Five: The Conquest

1. FREE, *op. cit.,* p. 125.

2. PFEIFFER, *op. cit.,* pp. 290-293.

3. FREE, *op. cit.,* p. 126.

4. KATHLEEN KENYON, *Archeology in the Holy Land* (New York: Frederick A. Praeger, 1960), pp. 104-110.

5. FINNEGAN, *op. cit.,* pp. 139-159.

6. KENYON, *op. cit.,* p. 210.

7. *Ibid.,* p. 211.

8. FINNEGAN, *op. cit.,* pp. 164, 167.

9. KENYON, *op. cit.,* p. 207.

Chapter Six: The Period of the Judges

1. FREE, *op. cit.,* p. 148.

2. FINNEGAN, *op. cit.,* p. 160.

3. *Ibid.,* pp. 164-167.

4. PFEIFFER, *op. cit.,* pp. 518-522.

5. FREE, *op. cit.,* p. 65.

Chapter Seven: The United Kingdom

1. J. A. THOMPSON, *Archaeology and the New Testament* (Grand Rapids, Mich.: Eerdmans, 1960) , pp. 76-77.

2. UNGER, *Archaeology and the Old Testament,* pp. 199-200.

3. FINNEGAN, *op. cit.,* p. 167.

4. UNGER, *Archaeology and the Old Testament,* p. 215.

5. THOMPSON, *Archaeology and the Old Testament* (Grand Rapids, Mich.: Eerdmans, 1959) , p. 79.

6. ERNEST WRIGHT, *Biblical Archaeology* (Philadelphia: Westminster, 1960) , pp. 136-140.

7. *Ibid.,* p. 135.

8. FREE, *op. cit.,* p. 170.

Chapter Eight: The Divided Kingdom

1. WRIGHT, *Biblical Archaeology,* pp. 152-153.

2. KENYON, *op. cit.,* pp. 266-268.

3. PFEIFFER, *op. cit.,* p. 396.

4. WRIGHT, *Biblical Archaeology,* pp. 169-171.

Chapter Nine: The Christian Era

1. J. B. PRITCHARD, "The 1951 Campaign at Herodian Jericho," *Bulletin of the American Schools of Oriental Research,* October, 1951, pp. 14-15.

2. THOMPSON, *Archaeology and the New Testament,* pp. 79-80.

3. MERRILL F. UNGER, *Archaeology and the New Testament* (Grand Rapids, Mich.: Zondervan, 1962), p. 98.

4. *Ibid.,* pp. 148-150.

5. PFEIFFER, *op. cit.,* pp. 287-289.

6. UNGER, *Archaeology of the New Testament,* p. 58.

7. *Ibid.,* p. 121.

8. FREE, *op. cit.,* pp. 294-295.

9. *Ibid.,* p. 306.

Chapter Ten: The Dead Sea Scrolls

1. WRIGHT, *Biblical Archaeology*, p. 213.

2. R. K. HARRISON, *The Dead Sea Scrolls* (New York: Harper, 1961), pp. 3-5.

3. *Ibid.*, p. 4.

4. *Ibid.*, p. 7.

5. UNGER, *Archaeology of the New Testament*, p. 81.

6. WRIGHT, *Biblical Archaeology*, pp. 213-217.

7. G. LANKESTER HARDING, *The Antiquities of Jordan* (New York: Crowell, 1960), pp. 179-183.

8. HARRISON, *op. cit.*, pp. 73-74.

9. *Ibid.*, pp. 75-77.

10. *Ibid.*, pp. 82-83.

11. *Ibid.*, pp. 11-15.

BIBLIOGRAPHY

ALBRIGHT, WILLIAM, *Archaeology and the Religion of Israel.* Johns Hopkins Press, Baltimore, Md., 1942.

––– *The Archaeology of Palestine.* Penguin Books Inc., Baltimore, Md., 1949.

––– *From Stone Age to Christianity.* Johns Hopkins Press, Baltimore, Md., 1940.

BARTON, GEORGE, *Archaeology and the Bible.* American Sunday School Union, Philadelphia, Pa., 1937.

BURROWS, MILLAR, *The Dead Sea Scrolls.* The Viking Press, New York, N.Y., 1955.

––– *What Mean These Stones,* American School of Oriental Research, New Haven, Conn., 1944.

FINNEGAN, JACK, *Light from the Ancient Past.* Princeton University Press, Princeton, N.J., 1959. (rev. ed.)

FREE, JOSEPH P., *Archaeology and Bible History.* Van Kampen Press, Wheaton, Ill., 1950.

GARSTANG, JOHN, *Joshua, Judges.* Constable, London, 1931.

GLUECK, NELSON, *The Other Side of the Jordan.* American School of Oriental Research, New Haven, Conn., 1940.

––– *Rivers in the Desert.* Farrar, Straus and Cudahy, Inc., New York, N.Y., 1957.

––– *The River Jordan.* Westminster Press, Philadelphia, Pa., 1946.

GORDON, CYRUS, *The World of the Old Testament.* Doubleday & Co., Inc., Garden City, New York, 1958.

HAMILTON, FLOYD E., *The Basis of Christian Belief.* Harper & Brothers, New York, N.Y., 1946.

HARDING, G. LANKESTER, *The Antiquities of Jordan.* Thomas Y. Crowell Co., New York, N.Y., 1959.

HARRISON, R. K., *Archaeology of the New Testament*. Association Press, New York, N.Y., 1964.

——— *The Dead Sea Scrolls*. Harper & Brothers, New York, N.Y., 1961.

KENYON, FREDERICK, *The Bible and Archeology*. Harper & Brothers, New York, N.Y., 1940.

KENYON, KATHLEEN M., *Beginning in Archaeology*. Frederick A. Praeger, Inc., New York, N.Y., 1952.

——— *Archaeology in the Holy Land*. Frederick A. Praeger, Inc., New York, N.Y., 1960.

KELSO, JAMES, *Archaeology and Our Old Testament Contemporaries*. Zondervan Publishing House, Grand Rapids, Mich., 1966.

McCOWN, C. C., *The Ladder of Progress in Palestine*. Harper & Brothers, New York, N.Y., 1943.

PETRIE, FLINDERS, *Palestine and Israel*. Society for Promoting Christian Knowledge, London, England, 1934.

PFEIFFER, CHARLES F., *The Biblical World*. Baker Book House, Grand Rapids, Mich., 1966.

PRITCHARD, JAMES, *Ancient Near Eastern Texts Relating to the Old Testament*. Princeton University Press, Princeton, N.J., 1955.

THOMPSON, J. A., *The Bible and Archeology*. William B. Eerdmans Publishing Company, Grand Rapids, Michigan, 1958.

UNGER, MERRILL F., *Archaeology and the Old Testament*. Zondervan Publishing House, Grand Rapids, Mich., 1954.

——— *Archaeology and the New Testament*. Zondervan Publishing House, Grand Rapids, Mich., 1962.

WEGENER, G. S., *6000 Years of the Bible*. Harper & Brothers, New York, N.Y., 1963.

WOOLLEY, LEONARD, *Ur of the Chaldees*. Charles Scribner's Sons, New York, N.Y., 1930.

——— *Digging Up the Past*. Charles Scribner's Sons, New York, N.Y., 1931.

WRIGHT, G. ERNEST, *Biblical Archaeology*. Westminster Press, Philadelphia, Pa., 1957.

——— *Biblical Archaeology*, Abridged Edition. Westminster Press, Philadelphia, Pa., 1960.

——— and FILSON, F. V., *The Westminster Historical Atlas to the Bible*. Westminster Press, Philadelphia, Pa., 1945.

INDEX

BIBLE REFERENCES